EXPLORERS

PIONEERS WHO BROKE
NEW BOUNDARIES

EXPLORERS
PIONEERS WHO BROKE NEW BOUNDARIES

By
Richard Platt

Consultant
Peter Chrisp

A Dorling Kindersley Book

Dorling  Kindersley

LONDON, NEW YORK, SYDNEY, DELHI,
PARIS, MUNICH, and JOHANNESBURG

Editor Sadie Smith
Art Editor Dawn Davies-Cook
Senior Editor Fran Jones
Senior Art Editor Marcus James
Category Publisher Jayne Parsons
Managing Art Editor Jacquie Gulliver
US Editors Gary Werner and Margaret Parrish
Picture Researcher Brenda Clynch
DK Pictures Rachel Hilford
Production Erica Rosen
DTP Designers Matthew Ibbotson,
Louise Paddick

First American Edition, 2001

01 02 03 04 05 10 9 8 7 6 5 4 3 2 1

Published in the United States by
DK Publishing, Inc.
95 Madison Avenue
New York, New York 10016

Copyright © 2001 Dorling Kindersley Limited

A cataloging-in-Publication record for this title is available from the Library of Congress.
ISBN 0-7894-7973-7 (hb)
ISBN 0-7894-7974-5 (pb)

Reproduced by Colourscan, Singapore
Printed and bound by L.E.G.O., Italy

See our complete catalog at

www.dk.com

CONTENTS

INTRODUCTION

Explorers are daring travelers in unknown lands. They face danger, even death, on their journeys. They come back as heroes – sometimes laden with treasure. But all explorers return with something more valuable than gold. They bring back knowledge, exotic tales of far-off places, and most important of all, directions on how to find those places again.

This book tells the fascinating story of exploration. You can follow explorers' journeys by sea, river, land, and ice. You'll learn how they climbed the world's highest peaks, how they dived to the ocean's depths, and how they soared high into space. You'll also find out why they did it.

Curiosity is perhaps the oldest reason for exploring. It's natural to wonder what's on the other side of the next hill. Explorers are just more curious than most of us – they wonder what's on the other side of the world.

Greed drove some to start their journeys – travel seemed an easy way to find wealth. A few did discover riches, though only

IN THE 13TH CENTURY THE CHINESE EMPEROR ORDERED A FLEET OF SHIPS TO BE BUILT FOR TRADE AND EXPLORATION.

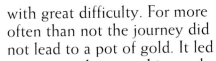

with great difficulty. For more often than not the journey did not lead to a pot of gold. It led to hunger, shipwreck, disease, and often death and disaster.

Glory was another reason for exploring. Those who discovered – or conquered – new lands became famous for their deeds, and often had lands or stretches of sea named after them. Many people also made great journeys in the name of religion. Christian missionaries, for example, aimed to take the story of the Bible to the people of Africa.

The story of exploration is a long and exciting one. For those of you who want to explore the subject in more detail, there are black Log On "boxes" that appear throughout the book. These addresses will direct you to some exciting websites where you can find out even more about the amazing story of exploration.

FIRST FOOTPRINTS

Who were the first explorers? Where did they come from, and where did they go? Exploration may have begun two million years ago, so you'd think there would be no traces left of the earliest explorers. Surprisingly, we do know a little about them – we can even guess what they were eating as they made the first amazing cross-continental journeys.

Let's make tracks!
The first explorers probably came from Africa, for this is where human life began. Most scientists now accept that all the world's people have descended from apelike ancestors who lived in Africa's forests more than 2 million years ago. These advanced apes fed on seeds, roots, fruits, and a little meat – perhaps worms and grubs, and the leftovers of the meals of ferocious hunting animals.

From studies of their bones and a trail of stone tools we know that a million years later the descendants of these hominids (nearly-humans) began to travel. Some of them started to spread out

AT FIRST, OUR ANCESTORS STAYED WHERE FAMILIAR FRUITS AND VEGETABLES WERE EASY FOR THEM TO FIND.

of the forests and explore the open plains of Africa.

Meat and mobility
As these hominids left the shadows of the forest, those who had learned to eat more meat got a head start on their vegetarian chums. On the plains the familiar fruits and root foods were scarce – especially in dry years. But there were always plenty of animals roaming the plains and grasslands. By eating more meat these first explorers had a food supply they could find over long distances, enabling them to travel and find their food where they pleased.

WE KNOW THAT AFRICA WAS THE HOME OF THE FIRST EXPLORERS, BUT EXPERTS STILL ARGUE OVER WHICH WAY THEY WENT, AND WHEN THEY TRAVELED. NEW EVIDENCE IS CONSTANTLY BEING FOUND.

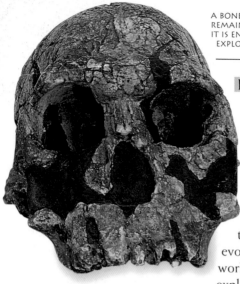

A BONE JIGSAW PUZZLE IS ALL THAT REMAINS OF EARLY HUMANS, BUT IT IS ENOUGH TO TELL US THAT THEY EXPLORED MUCH OF EAST AFRICA.

Following the clues
Which way did the first explorers go? Scientists in search of human origins would love to know. To answer this question they must follow a trail of bone and stone tools in order to piece together how humans evolved and spread across the world. From the bones of the explorers themselves, scientists try and figure out who went where, and when.

However, the clues tell a confusing story. It's clear that

Out of Africa
From their homeland, the hominids probably plodded north. Within 25,000 years

THE FIRST HUMANS TO EXPLORE WERE ALSO THE FIRST TO USE FIRE

we know they had explored as far as Southeast Asia. Pretty slow going? Perhaps it was. But unlike later explorers, these travelers were not competing to be the first or the fastest. They even stopped and raised families on the way. The earliest travelers advanced perhaps 6 miles (10 km) in each generation – that's approximately two paces a day!

the first explorers came from Africa, but from there, the exact route they followed is almost impossible to trace. Even experts can't agree whether there was just one wave of travelers from Africa or two. What is clear, though, is that by 250,000 years ago, modern humans had explored almost every corner of Africa, Asia, and Europe.

LOG ON...
Find out about early humans at:
www.leakeyfoundation.org/

American dream

Reaching the American continents was tricky. Wide oceans separate North and South America from Asia, Africa, and Europe – except at one point. At Asia's top right corner and North America's top left corner the continents almost touch. The gap between them, the Bering Strait, is now 53 miles (85 km) wide. However, some 11,300 years ago the strait was dry land. The world's climate was very much colder then, and thick sheets of ice covered vast areas. These locked up water from the oceans, lowering sea levels and creating a "land bridge" between Asia and North America. Explorers flocked across with their families and found a land of limitless food. Huge mammals, such as woolly mammoths, roamed the continent. Their bellies bulging with mammoth meat, these first Americans gradually moved south. After 5,5000 years they had succeeded in exploring and colonizing virtually all of North and South America.

STONE TOOLS FOUND WITH HUMAN FOSSILS WERE PROBABLY USED BY EARLY MAN FOR BUTCHERING MEAT.

RICHARD LEAKEY AND HIS PARENTS, LOUIS AND MARY, DUG UP SOME OF THE EARLIEST HUMAN REMAINS IN EAST AFRICA.

EASTERN PIONEERS

When the emperor says "Explore," you don't ask questions. You get your boots on – fast! The first explorers from Asia began their travels at the emperor's command, voyaging far from their homes in China's great empire. In their tracks came pilgrims on religious voyages of discovery.

CHINESE
SILK

Mission impossible

Chang Chi'en, the commander of the Chinese palace guard, started the trek west more than 2,000 years ago. His emperor chose him to lead 100 men across central Asia. Their mission was to arrange a treaty with tribes that would help China defeat wandering Hun warriors. However, Chang Chi'en was a hopeless negotiator. Not only did he fail to obtain a treaty, he was also held prisoner by the Huns for 10 years! But,

EARLY EASTERN TRAVELERS COVERED VAST DISTANCES OVER STEEP MOUNTAINS. THE XINJIANG RANGE IN NORTHWEST CHINA OVERLOOKS THE FAMOUS SILK ROAD.

he was a great explorer. He got as far as Samarkand (now in Uzbekistan) and returned via Tibet, with news of a great western sea – it was the Mediterranean Sea.

Tales of far-off lands

Chang Chi'en's journey showed that travel to the west was possible. The country of Li-chien that he described was the city-state of Rome. Already powerful when Chang Chi'en heard of it, Rome would soon rule the whole of the Mediterranean area and lands far beyond. This pioneering journey helped to open up a trail across Asia. It was called the Silk Road after the valuable cloth that traveling merchants carried. The Silk Road was to become the main trade route between East and West for nearly 1,500 years.

Mighty Khan

Travelers on the Silk Road were constantly in danger from roaming bandits. This trade route only became safer in the 13th century, when the Mongol people, led by Genghis Khan, conquered China. The Mongols took control of much of the land through which the Silk Road passed, ridding it of bandits who terrorized traders.

THE MONGOL WARRIORS OF GENGHIS KHAN RAIDED AS FAR WEST AS IRAN AND IRAQ.

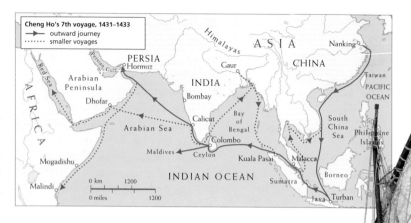

Cheng Ho's 7th voyage, 1431–1433
→ outward journey
⋯⋯ smaller voyages

ON CHENG HO'S 7TH VOYAGE, HIS HUGE FLEET CRISSCROSSED THE SOUTH CHINA SEA, THE BAY OF BENGAL, AND THE INDIAN OCEAN.

Genghis Khan himself had a streak of the explorer in him. After he had "explored" his native Mongolia, all opposition to his power crumbled. His brutal "exploration" of China brought half the world under the control of the Mongols.

despite the fact that he was 71 years old. He set off in 1219.

Ch'ang-ch'un's journey took 14 months, on ox cart, horseback, and on foot. His group forged raging rivers and traveled through deep snow in

GENGHIS KHAN MEANS "UNIVERSAL LEADER"

Quest for the West
Once in power, Genghis Khan encouraged exploration of a more peaceful sort. He ordered philosopher Ch'ang-ch'un on a fact-finding mission to central Asia. Ch'ang-ch'un was wise enough not to refuse the job,

high mountain passes. They saw many novelties including a cotton field. Cotton was then unknown in China and Ch'ang-ch'un believed that it was farmed by planting sheep and plucking the wool from the crop of

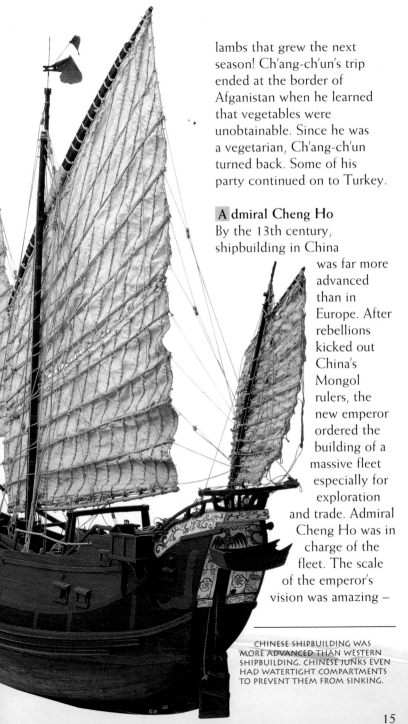

lambs that grew the next season! Ch'ang-ch'un's trip ended at the border of Afganistan when he learned that vegetables were unobtainable. Since he was a vegetarian, Ch'ang-ch'un turned back. Some of his party continued on to Turkey.

Admiral Cheng Ho

By the 13th century, shipbuilding in China was far more advanced than in Europe. After rebellions kicked out China's Mongol rulers, the new emperor ordered the building of a massive fleet especially for exploration and trade. Admiral Cheng Ho was in charge of the fleet. The scale of the emperor's vision was amazing —

CHINESE SHIPBUILDING WAS MORE ADVANCED THAN WESTERN SHIPBUILDING. CHINESE JUNKS EVEN HAD WATERTIGHT COMPARTMENTS TO PREVENT THEM FROM SINKING.

15

there were 63 ships in the fleet, with a crew of 27,000. The largest ships were 400 ft (122 m) long and 160 ft (50 m) wide. Straining on their nine masts were sails so vast that they looked like great red clouds when seen from a distance.

CHENG HO BROUGHT A GIRAFFE BACK FROM AFRICA AS A GIFT FOR HIS EMPEROR.

Epic journeys

Under Cheng Ho's command, the emperor's fleet sailed south as far as Java in Indonesia, across the Bay of Bengal and the Indian Ocean. The ships visited the Persian Gulf and the Red Sea, and sailed down Africa's east coast to Malindi (see page 14).

In all, Cheng Ho's treasure fleet made seven voyages. They brought back zebras and giraffes from Africa. In exchange, they left enough porcelain bowls to tile the dome of an African mosque (Muslim temple). On the last spectacular voyage the fleet sailed the equivalent of half-way around the world.

Holy hikers

It was religion that really gave a push to explorers from the East. Buddhist monk Fa Hsien made the first recorded pilgrimage (holy journey) from China in

ad 400. His travels, which lasted 14 years, took him across Central Asia and south to the island of Ceylon (now Sri Lanka). Two centuries later another monk, Hsüan Tsang, traced a similar route. In the featureless Gobi desert he would have gotten lost if

FEW MODERN BUDDHIST MONKS MAKE PILGRIMAGES AS LONG AS FA HSIEN'S.

he had not followed a train of horse dung and bones of unlucky travelers who had gone before him!

The world of Islam

Pilgrims of another great religion explored much more of the East. After the prophet Mohammed founded Islam in the desert lands of the Arabian peninsula in the 7th century AD, the religion spread rapidly. One of the five pillars (religious duties) of Islam is to make a haj – a pilgrimage to Mecca, Mohammed's birthplace. The haj gave

Muslims (followers of Islam) a real taste for travel.

The 10th-century scholar Al Mas'udi (d. AD 957) spent all his adult life traveling, aiming to visit every Islamic country in the world. Not much remains of the detailed account he wrote of his trips, but the journals of some later Arab travelers have survived.

Al-Idrisi, who lived from 1100–1166, worked for the Norman king, Roger II of Sicily. He was also a keen explorer. Al-Idrisi traveled widely in Africa, the Middle East, and the Canary Islands.

WHEN IBN BATTÚTA DESCRIBED THE PYRAMIDS 700 YEARS AGO, THEY WERE ALREADY A FAMOUS TOURIST ATTRACTION.

Muslim globetrotter

Ibn Battúta (d.1304) was the greatest of all Muslim explorers. A scholar and a qadi (religious court judge) he spent nearly 30 years traveling. To repeat his amazing journey today, you would need to visit 44 countries.

In one of them – Egypt – he missed a "must-see" sight, the famous pyramids, which, in a rare blunder, he described as cone-shaped. Ibn Battúta's descriptions of his wanderings give a vivid glimpse of life in the Middle Ages. He set off almost penniless, but through the generosity of the people he visited he became a rich man.

The journeys were not without problems, however. Just before reaching India, he and his companions were attacked by bandits. They fought them off bravely, killing several. They hung the severed heads of those they had killed from the walls of a nearby fort to warn other bandits of the risks they took.

In Delhi, the sultan made him ambassador to China. He loaded Ibn Battúta with treasures and sent him on his way with 100 fine horses and 200 women. However, his wealth did not last long – after just a day's journey his vast

LIKE IBN BATTÚTA, TODAY'S PILGRIMS WALK SEVEN TIMES AROUND THE KA'BAH – THE SHRINE AT THE CENTER OF MECCA'S GREAT MOSQUE.

19

caravan was attacked, and he lost everything!

Travelers' tall tales

Ibn Battúta's journal of his wanderings reads like a fairy tale, and it's sometimes impossible to tell truth from fantasy. For example, in Delhi he described with amazement the stunts of yogis (holy men expert in yoga): "The sultan

When he finally gave up his wanderings, he had travelled 75,000 miles (120,000 km) – the equivalent of three times around the world.

Arab seamanship

As part of his grand tour, Ibn Battúta was going to sail from Yemen to India, but changed his plan when he saw the leaky ship provided for him! It's

IBN BATTÚTA'S JOURNEYS TOOK ALMOST 30 YEARS

sent for me…and I found him with two of these yogis. One of them squatted on the ground, then rose into the air above our heads, still sitting. I was so astonished and frightened that I fell to the floor in a faint."

After yet more traveling (and surviving two shipwrecks and an attack by pirates), Ibn Battúta reached Sumatra in Indonesia. While there, he witnessed slaves cutting off their own heads in a tradition which demonstrated loyalty to their sultan masters.

THIS MUD-BRICK MOSQUE IN DJENNÉ, MALI, IS VERY SIMILAR TO THE BUILDING WHERE IBN BATTÚTA WORSHIPPED.

possible he had high safety standards, for Arab ships and seamen were usually among the world's best. Their navigation (direction finding) methods were more advanced than those used in Europe. Among the instruments they used was a kamal. This was little more than a wooden square and a piece of string. Nevertheless, it allowed Arab seamen in the Indian Ocean to judge how far they had sailed north or south – at a time when most European sailors were relying on guesswork.

THIS ARAB QUADRANT FROM THE 19TH CENTURY IS A DEVELOPMENT FROM THE SIMPLER KAMAL.

EUROPE EXPLORES

If you had lived in India 2,400 years ago, or in the Americas 400 years ago, you might not have been too pleased to be "discovered" by an explorer. For when explorers from Europe first visited these countries, sightseeing was not their only goal. They wanted to conquer the people they met and claim their lands. When the people they met opposed them, these "explorers" often used force to get what they wanted.

Roaming Europeans
Many European explorers thought that theirs was the only "civilized" continent. They treated people they met on their travels outside of Europe as savages or animals. Of course,

ITALIAN EXPLORER CHRISTOPHER COLUMBUS MEETS THE NATIVES IN SAN SALVADOR, OCTOBER 12, 1492.

Europeans were not the only explorers who exploited the people and lands of the countries they visited. Asian and Arab explorers did the same. But for some 2,000 years, European explorers were the most daring, wide-ranging, and successful.

Alexander the Great explorer

One of the first – and still the greatest – of the European explorers was Alexander III, exploring army moved on east, to Pakistan and India, and then back to Persia.

Alexander's explorations came to a sudden end in 323 BC, when he died after a particularly wild banquet. Nobody would explore (or party) quite as enthusiastically as Alexander for nearly 14 centuries.

Raiders or explorers?

Like Alexander, the Viking people were at first more

ALEXANDER FOUNDED 32 CITIES AND NAMED THEM ALL ALEXANDRIA

the 4th century BC king of Macedonia in the Greek Empire. He's best known as Alexander the Great. But he did not earn the "great" nickname because he was a great explorer. Conquest was what he did best – exploration was just a sideline for this king.

Alexander sent surveyors ahead of his troops. What they found not only made invasion easier, but it also added greatly to knowledge of the world beyond Europe. Alexander and his troops went to Turkey and Persia (now Iran), and they marched through the Middle East to Egypt before returning to Persia. Then Alexander's

interested in plunder than discovery. In the 9th century AD, these sassy Scandinavian seafarers began raiding towns and monasteries on the coasts of Europe's North Sea. As their homelands got too crowded for comfort, they turned from raiding to exploration.

By AD 874, they had sailed their lightweight, flexible ships to Iceland. A century later they were founding colonies in Greenland. Then, about a thousand years ago, Viking "Lucky" Leif Eriksson sailed on west and south to discover a new land. He called it Vinland. Today we know it as Newfoundland – Canada's most eastern corner.

How do we know all this? Because the Vikings were incurable boasters and loved to tell sagas (stories) about their fathers' exciting journeys. Archaeologists confirmed the sagas about Vinland in 1963, when they dug up the remains of a Viking village in Newfoundland.

known world. To trade with China and other Asian countries you could go only one way – east. But, going east was getting harder. The power of the Mongol people (see page 13) was crumbling, and without their policing, the trade route to China was too dangerous. Also, Islamic people controlled the eastern Mediterranean and stopped the Christian merchants of Europe from trading further east.

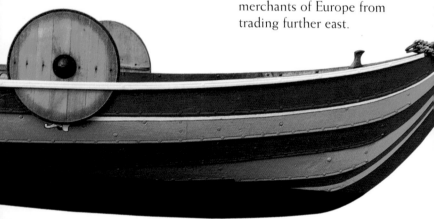

VIKING SHIPS HAD NO CABINS. WHEN FAR FROM LAND, EXPLORERS SLEPT ON THE OPEN DECKS OF THEIR LONGSHIPS.

The Vikings never made North America their home – to them "Vinland" became little more than a memory.

Routes east

To other Europeans, the Americas simply did not exist. It may seem extraordinary, but in the 15th century Europe lay at the western edge of the

Armchair navigator

Portugal's Prince Henry looked for a solution to this difficult problem. From 1420, he sponsored voyages south along Africa's western coast. It was a bold idea, for maps of Africa ended halfway down the bulgy part at the top left. His imaginative ideas earned him the nickname "the Navigator" (even though he never did much navigating himself).

Later, he began to dream that

LOG ON...
Read more about Vikings at:
www.mnh.si.edu/vikings/

if Portugal's little ships went far enough south, they would be able to sail around the bottom of Africa and find a sea route to the East. Sadly, Henry died in 1460, long before his dream of a sea route to Asia came true. Portuguese navigator Bartolomeu Dias was the first to sail around Africa's Cape of Good Hope in 1488. Once he'd shown the way, of course, anybody could do it. Eleven years later Vasco da Gama went further, crossing the Indian Ocean to trade with India (see pages 32–33).

First stop America

Italian mariner Christopher Columbus had a different idea. He wanted to sail across the Atlantic to Asia. However, what Columbus didn't know was that there was a small obstacle to navigation – the Americas. He made his historic voyage in 1492, and hit an obstacle right in the very middle – the Caribbean islands. Thinking he was nearing India, he called them the West Indies. The inhabitants became known as – you guessed it – Indians.

Golden age of plunder

Columbus' voyage marked the beginning of European exploration of this "New World," as the Americas were

---

BARTOLOMEU DIAS NAMED AFRICA'S TIP "THE CAPE OF STORMS." HIS KING THOUGHT THIS MADE IT SOUND TERRIBLE, SO HE CHANGED "STORMS" TO "GOOD HOPE."

known. Those who followed spread out from the Caribbean to the American mainland.

In Mexico, Spaniard Hernán Cortés discovered the Aztecs, a warlike people whose capital was richly decorated with gold.

High in the Andes Mountains of Peru another Spaniard, Francisco Pizarro, found the Inca civilization. The Incas had a culture at least as advanced as that of Spain, and like the Aztecs, they made beautiful works of art from precious metals. Dazzled by the gold and silver, Cortés and Pizarro became conquistadors (conquerors). Between 1520 and 1540 they plundered the wealth of the Aztecs and Incas, killed or enslaved their people, and took their lands.

Some distance north, British adventurers had named North America's Atlantic shore New England, and the French began to explore New France (now

AT THE GATES OF HIS CAPITAL, TENOCHTITLAN, MEXICO'S EMPEROR MONTEZUMAH WELCOMED SPANISH CONQUISTADOR HERNAN CORTÉS.

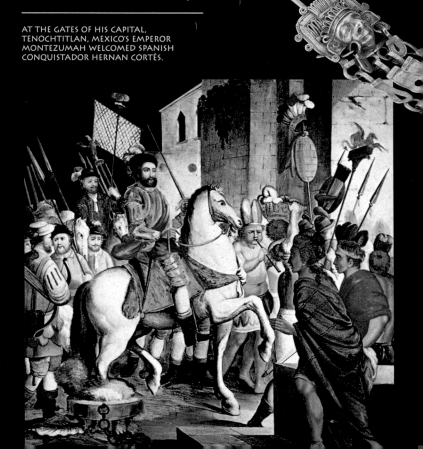

Canada). As the Europeans explored the vast North American continent, they claimed the "empty" lands they found as their own. When the Native American people who already lived there opposed them, the settlers drove the Native Americans from the land with guns.

The last continent…
After the Americas, what was there left to explore? Mapmakers were vague about the south of the Earth. They thought there must be something there to balance up the North Pole. So they

DISEASES, SUCH AS FLU, BROUGHT TO THE AMERICAS BY EUROPEAN SETTLERS MAY HAVE KILLED NINE IN EVERY TEN NATIVE AMERICANS.

MEXICO'S SPANISH CONQUERORS MELTED DOWN BEAUTIFUL AZTEC ART INTO EASY-TO-CARRY GOLD BRICKS.

scribbled in an imaginary continent, and called it *Terra Australis* (southern land).

Nobody really knew what was there until 1616, when Dutch sailors landed in Western Australia. Dutchman Abel Tasman penciled in the left-hand side and the top of

the continent a quarter of a century later. Much to his dismay, Tasman found "nothing profitable, only poor naked people" in Australia.

The English, however, came up with an ingenious use for this distant land – they used it as a prison! In 1788, the British claimed New South Wales as their own and shipped out all their undesirables to a life of hard labor in this desolate land.

Australia wasn't quite the last continent to be explored. Antarctica, an ice-covered landmass farther south still, remained a white blob until the early 20th century. Mapmakers only filled in the more remote parts of the other continents around the same time.

SEA VOYAGES

The world's first ocean sailors did not dare travel out of sight of land. But some 4,500 years ago, Egyptian and Greek sailors learned to find their way across open sea by following stars, tides, and winds. Improvements in ship design and route-finding methods made longer voyages possible. By the 16th century, European mariners were skilled and confident enough to sail around the world.

Early navigation
Egyptian and European sailors were not the only adventurous ones, they just left behind the best descriptions of their

Nile boats and sails
Around the Mediterranean, it's easier to trace how early ocean explorers made their voyages. Pictures and models from Egypt

MANY SAILORS BELIEVED IN HUGE, SNAKELIKE OCEAN MONSTERS

journeys. Elsewhere in the world, we have to piece together the story of ocean exploration like a jigsaw puzzle. Polynesian people, for instance, left no written records of their long voyages across the open Pacific. But we know they made the trips by tracing the spread of their language and distinctive pottery.

suggest that sailing ships were in use on the Nile as long ago as 2,500 BC. Similar ships built on the island of Crete crossed the open sea to trade with Egypt. These early ships had oars as well as sails, to provide power when the wind dropped. The calm waters of the Mediterranean Sea made sailing easy for the crews of these craft. But when early mariners left the safety of the sea, and ventured out into the cold Atlantic Ocean in the 6th century, they played it safe and stuck close to the European and African coasts.

LOG ON...
www.nmm.ac.uk/education/
fact_agesail.html

L ongboats and strong ships
A few were more daring. In the 9th century, the Viking people sailed their sleek longboats across the stormy North Atlantic (see page 23). But real long-distance ocean sailing didn't start for another 600 years when new inventions made it safer. The shipbuilders of southern Europe created caravels – strong, three-masted ships that could stand the harshest gales. The mariners who sailed them relied on navigation instruments copied from Chinese and Arab navigators.

T o the east by sea
The Portuguese and Spanish were the first Europeans to bring these advances together, and in the early 15th century, they started making longer voyages. Inspired by Henry the Navigator (see page 24) they began to search for a sea route to Asia – the

RUMORS OF SHIP-EATING MONSTERS MADE MARINERS FEAR LONG SEA VOYAGES.

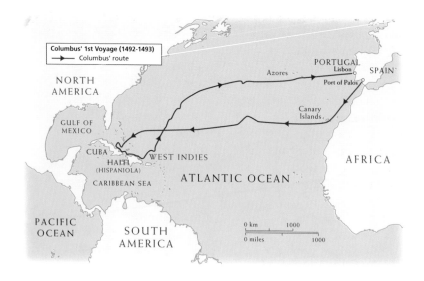

Columbus' 1st Voyage (1492-1493)
— Columbus' route

NORTH AMERICA

PORTUGAL
Lisbon
SPAIN
Azores
Port of Palos

GULF OF MEXICO

Canary Islands

CUBA
HAITI
(HISPANIOLA)
WEST INDIES
CARIBBEAN SEA
ATLANTIC OCEAN

AFRICA

PACIFIC OCEAN

SOUTH AMERICA

0 km   1000
0 miles   1000

THE ROUTE THAT COLUMBUS PIONEERED BECAME THE STANDARD SEA-LANE FOR SHIPS SAILING TO THE CARIBBEAN.

source of valuable silks and spices. One sailor, Italian-born Christopher Columbus, had an outrageous plan. He believed Asia was less than three weeks sailing across the Atlantic.

Bankers and navigation experts thought Columbus' plan was crazy and refused to give him money to fund the voyage, so Columbus went to Spain to raise money for the trip. In 1492, Spain's rulers, King Ferdinand and Queen Isabella, agreed to support him. In return, Columbus promised to bring them back gold.

Columbus' first voyage

That fall Columbus sailed due west from the Canary Islands with three ships and about

VALUABLE SPICES, SUCH AS GINGER, LURED TRADERS TO MAKE THEIR WAY EASTWARD.

100 nervous Spanish seamen. Knowing that his crew would get more anxious the farther they sailed from Spain, Columbus lied about how far they had gone. He wrote in his diary, "...Today I [sailed] 180 miles...I recorded only 144 in order not to alarm the sailors."

Arrival in San Salvador

On October 11, after a month-long voyage, they sighted land. It was San Salvador in the Bahamas – or was it Samana Cay in the eastern Bahamas? Experts have suggested nine different places as possible landing sites, and to this day we don't know exactly where Columbus landed. Neither, for that matter, did he.

Columbus believed that Asia was just around the next corner. For four months he hunted for it (and for gold), visiting Cuba and Haiti, before returning to Spain. In all, Christopher Columbus made four voyages across the Atlantic Ocean.

Longest voyage

Columbus hadn't gotten what he wanted from the trip – a sea route to Asia. Nor had he "discovered" America. Asian people had found it thousands of years earlier, and the first Europeans there – the Vikings – beat Columbus by five centuries. But, Columbus had done two amazing things – he had made an ocean crossing four times farther than the European record, and he had "decoded" the wind systems of the Atlantic. Columbus found a southern

ON LANDING, COLUMBUS WROTE IN HIS LOGBOOK "I WENT ASHORE IN THE SHIP'S BOAT...I UNFURLED THE ROYAL BANNER."

route where the winds blew ships out to the Americas, and a northern route where the wind blew ships home. Thanks to his discovery, European people were able to explore and settle in the Americas.

Portugal explores

In 1497, four years after Columbus returned, the Portuguese mariner Vasco da Gama set off in the other direction – east. His goal was to sail around Africa to India. His three ships reached the Cape of Good Hope in November, but gales there battered the ships, driving them back. Da Gama used shock treatment to control the terrified crew. He tossed the ship's charts into the sea, saying to his men "I do not need a navigator, because God alone is our master…" Having shown the sailors that there was no

VASCO DA GAMA WAS CHOSEN FOR THE VOYAGE TO INDIA AFTER HIS FATHER, THE PORTUGUESE KING'S FIRST CHOICE, DIED.

turning back, da Gama sailed on up Africa's eastern coast, stopping to trade cheap trinkets with the coastal people. These wandering farmers had never seen anything quite like the Portuguese novelties. In exchange they offered cattle and drinking water.

SAILORS USED ASTROLABES TO GAUGE THEIR POSITION FROM THE SUN'S HEIGHT.

Cheap trade

Further up the coast, people were less impressed. They told him of much finer gifts

DE GAMA'S CHEAP GIFTS INSULTED HIS INDIAN HOST

brought by "white ghosts" who had visited years earlier in much larger ships (probably Cheng Ho's vast treasure fleet – see page 15).

Da Gama had other problems, too. Sailors' hands and feet had swollen, and their gums were bleeding. It was the first sign of a horrible disease called scurvy, which later attacked sailors on all long ocean journeys.

Disappointment in India

Despite these difficulties, Vasco da Gama crossed the Indian Ocean, reaching Calicut in India in May 1898.

The wealthy Hindu ruler welcomed da Gama, but his courtiers just laughed at the Portuguese when they presented the gifts they had brought – wash basins and rancid butter! These meager presents showed that da Gama was expecting to trade with simple savages.

It was obvious that he was not going to get the trade treaty he wanted in India. So Vasco da Gama limped home, losing a third of his crew to scurvy on the way.

Nevertheless, his trip opened the sea route to the east, and within 20 years the Portuguese

33

MAGELLAN SET OFF ON THE FIRST VOYAGE AROUND THE WORLD, BUT DIED BEFORE IT WAS COMPLETE.

talented navigator called Ferdinand Magellan. If Magellan could reach the Spice Islands of Asia (now called the Moluccas) by sailing west, he could claim them as Spanish – and kick out Spain's Portuguese rivals.

Magellan's fleet of five ships set sail in the fall of 1519. He reached the South American coast by November, turned left, and looked for "The Strait" (a sea passage leading to Asia).

controlled almost all Indian Ocean trade. He returned to India in 1502 with better weapons and stronger ships.

L and of opportunity?

You've probably gathered by now that Asia was a big deal. Columbus and his followers may have discovered a whole new continent, but who cared? To 16th-century Europeans, the "New World" was in the way between them and Asia. To them, America wasn't an opportunity, it was an obstacle.

M agellan to the rescue

To find a way around this inconvenient continent, Spain's King Charles hired a

T he Strait of Magellan

It took Magellan nearly a year to find what he was looking for. The bottom left-hand corner of the Atlantic Ocean (now called the Strait of Magellan after the famous seaman) turned out to be a dangerous, stormy channel through a maze of islands. Magellan was so relieved to sail through it that he wept with joy.

He should have saved his tears for later, because the worst part of the voyage was about to begin. The ocean he sailed into was calm (so calm

that he called it the Pacific),
but it was absolutely vast,
and they had no food left.
The crew ate sawdust, biscuits
soaked in rat urine, and rats.
Scurvy killed them by the
dozen. Magellan himself died
in a fight with native people
on a Pacific island.

Skeleton crew

Just two of the ships made
it to the Spice Islands. They
loaded up their ships with
spices and headed back to
Spain, without their captain.
However, only one succeeded
in crossing the Indian Ocean.

ONLY ONE OF MAGELLAN'S SHIPS, THE
VICTORIA, RETURNED TO SEVILLE. A
RECONSTRUCTION OF THIS SHIP IS
NOW ON DISPLAY THERE.

On board were just 17 of the
270 sailors who had set off
three years earlier. The ship
was leaking badly, the crew
looked like skeletons and were

Weird World

MAGELLAN'S CREW GOT HOME
ON A THURSDAY, YET THEIR
CALENDAR TOLD THEM IT WAS
WEDNESDAY! ALL AROUND-
THE-WORLD VOYAGERS LOSE
OR GAIN A DAY, DEPENDING
ON WHETHER THEY TRAVEL
EAST OR WEST.

"weaker than men have ever
been before." But they had
achieved something nobody
had ever done before. They
had sailed around the world.

The perils of sea travel

The awful experiences of
Magellan's crew were not
that unusual. Life on a
16th-century sailing ship
was tough, unpleasant,
and dangerous even
when things were going
according to plan.
When voyages went
wrong, as they often did,
a sailor's job became so
awful that death must have
seemed a sensible career move
by comparison.

The ships themselves made
life very difficult. They were
great for coastal cruising, but
crossing an ocean in one was
another story entirely. Ocean
explorers from Spain and
Portugal sailed tiny ships – all

35

ON THE RETURN JOURNEY, COLUMBUS'
SHIP WAS HIT BY A STORM SO SEVERE THAT
ALL THE CREW EXPECTED TO DIE.

three of Columbus' would fit
onto two tennis courts. With
100 men crowded on board,
living conditions were
cramped, and most of the crew
slept on the open deck. Their
clothes soon became filthy,

because washing them was
impossible, since clothes
soaked in salt water took so
long to dry.

The crew ate biscuits, salted
meat, cheese, and sometimes
beans. Unfortunately so did the
ship's rats and maggots, which
greatly outnumbered the
humans on board. While this
food lasted it made for filling,
but boring meals. When it ran
out sailors became anglers.
Magellan's men baited hooks
with white rags, which they
dangled just above the waves
to look like flying fish (but
only to a tuna). When fish
wouldn't bite, they ate the
ship's leather fittings. "We
soaked them for days in the sea,
then laid them a short time on

embers, and so we ate them."
If food was bad, water was even
worse – slime grew quickly in
water barrels. Wine and beer
kept better, and only when
these ran out did the seamen
quench their thirst with water.

Overcrowding and bad hygiene
caused deadly ship-fever
(typhus), and tropical diseases
spread rapidly. Falls from the
rigging broke limbs and backs,
crippling those few who
managed to survive the fall.

D isease of sailors
Lack of fresh fruits and
vegetables in the sailor's diet

F inding your way at sea
With all these hardships and
hazards, most of us would have
difficulty sailing across a pond,
let alone the Atlantic Ocean.

RATS WERE THE
CONSTANT
COMPANIONS
OF SAILORS ON
LONG VOYAGES.

caused scurvy. Sailors suffering
from scurvy had swollen, sore
limbs, bloody gums, and loose
teeth – and eventually died
of bleeding inside
their bodies. Scurvy
killed sailors on
long-distance
voyages until the
18th century, when
ships began to carry
lemons and limes.
Drinking their juice
supplied the sailors with
vitamin C which
prevented the disease.
Scurvy was not the only killer.

But we haven't even
mentioned the biggest
problem of ocean
sailing – finding
the way to the
next piece of
land when all
you can see
around you is sea!

ENGLISH CAPTAIN JOHN HAWKINS
SUGGESTED LEMON JUICE AS A SCURVY
CURE IN 1593, BUT 150 YEARS PASSED BEFORE
THE WORLD'S NAVIES TOOK HIS ADVICE.

OVER THE RAPIDS

To explore a vast unknown land, buy a boat! This is not such a strange idea. Land travel is costly, difficult, and often dangerous. Swamps, mountains, and canyons, trap unwary travelers and slow them down. Rivers on the other hand, are perfect highways. They are mostly flat and stretch from the heart of a continent all the way to the sea.

Explore by boat
The first European explorers of Africa realized that the fastest and easiest way to get around was on rivers – the Nile, the Niger, the Congo (Zaire), and the Zambesi.

MUNGO PARK'S EXPLORATIONS WERE DELAYED WHEN AN ARAB CHIEF IMPRISONED HIM FOR FOUR MONTHS.

The mystery river
Scotsman Mungo Park, one of the first successful explorers of Africa, was very open about his

MUNGO PARK'S AMBITION WAS TO BE A RICH AND FAMOUS EXPLORER

Africa's explorers had another reason for choosing river travel – they saw in Africa a chance to make money, and believed the rivers would provide merchants with a fast route to the African interior.

reasons for using rivers to explore Africa. At the beginning of his book *Travels Into the Interior of Africa* Park admitted his aim in exploration was "opening…new sources of wealth, and new channels of

LOG ON...
Read about Lewis and Clark at:
www.pbs.org/lewisandclark

commerce." Park began his travels in 1795, after the Africa Association of London paid for him to explore the Niger. This great river was a mystery – nobody was sure where it started or where it reached the sea. Park set off up the Gambia River by boat, then continued overland on horseback. He carried few clothes, food, and equipment, but by African standards he was a rich man and was often robbed. On one occasion bandits stripped him completely naked.

Park did reach the Niger, but far from unraveling its mystery, he had deepened it, for he discovered that the river flowed away from the nearest coastline, not toward it. When he realized that he could not trace the river's course on his own, he gave up his expedition and returned to England.

A second chance

In 1805, Park tried again. This time he took a huge expedition, including 34 soldiers. From the start the straggling group was a magnet for thieves. Many of

THE NIGER FLOWS THROUGH FIVE DIFFERENT COUNTRIES, EVENTUALLY REACHING THE SEA IN NIGERIA.

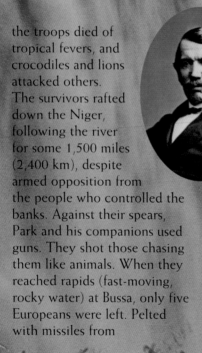

LIVINGSTONE'S ENGLISH NAME FOR THE VICTORIA FALLS STILL APPEARS IN EVERY ATLAS.

the troops died of tropical fevers, and crocodiles and lions attacked others. The survivors rafted down the Niger, following the river for some 1,500 miles (2,400 km), despite armed opposition from the people who controlled the banks. Against their spears, Park and his companions used guns. They shot those chasing them like animals. When they reached rapids (fast-moving, rocky water) at Bussa, only five Europeans were left. Pelted with missiles from the bank, Park attempted to run the river rapids. As the raft spun out of control, he and his companions jumped into the rushing water and drowned.

Cruel trade

After his first expedition, Mungo Park had left Africa on a slave ship and saw the terrible suffering of the human "cargo." Later, the cruelty of the slave trade attracted many campaigning explorers to Africa. Scottish missionary David Livingstone was one of them. Missionaries were people

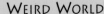

WEIRD WORLD
WHEN LIVINGSTONE DIED IN ZAMBIA, HIS AFRICAN SERVANTS BURIED HIS HEART AND PRESERVED HIS BODY IN SALT. IT TOOK NINE MONTHS TO CARRY IT TO THE COAST FOR TRANSPORT TO ENGLAND AND A HERO'S FUNERAL.

who traveled to spread their religious beliefs and set up schools in the local communities they visited.

Livingstone explores Africa

In 1841, Livingstone set off from Cape Town in South Africa to introduce Africans to three C's – Christianity, Commerce, and Civilization. Africans already had their own religions, were enthusiastic traders, and their continent was the home of several great empires. But, like other European explorers, Livingstone ignored this.

Livingstone's Christian beliefs inspired him to pursue a life of exploration. He traveled further into southern Africa than any white man had been before.

He crossed the Kalahari Desert and was the first European to see Lake Ngami. Livingstone traced the Zambezi River until he came to a great waterfall called Mosi Oa Tunya (smoke that thunders). He renamed it Victoria Falls, after the queen of England.

Stanley arrives

Livingstone's long, difficult, and often very dangerous explorations of southern Africa's rivers made him famous in Britain. When he

VICTORIA FALLS, ZIMBABWE

lost touch with "civilized" Europe in 1870, people feared for his safety. Welsh-American journalist Henry Stanley set off to find him. Leading a well-equipped and heavily armed convoy, he fought his way through wars and plagues to eventually find Livingstone at a place called Ujiji, on Lake Tanganyika in Zaire. He greeted the lost hero with the now-famous words "Doctor Livingstone, I presume?" – a stupid question, since Livingstone's face was well-known, and he was the only white man for miles.

Stanley's expedition brought Livingstone vital supplies, but the great explorer was a sick man. He died two years later while searching for the source of the Nile River.

Stanley continued with Livingstone's work, sailing 2,000 miles (3,200 km) down the Congo River to trace its route to the sea. However, he did not share Livingstone's respect for African people, and often blasted his way out of a tight spot with deadly gunfire.

Tracing Earth's longest river
Of all Africa's rivers, the Nile was both the most famous and the least understood. An

ancient civilization grew up in its valley, yet the Nile puzzled the Egyptians who relied on it. Where did the river come from? And why did it flood every year? According to legends, a mountain range called "The mountains of the Moon" fed the river with water.

Halfway along its length, the Nile forks into two branches. It was the west branch, the White Nile, that was the greatest mystery. By the mid-19th century, explorers had traced the White Nile through a great swamp called As-Sudd (barrier). Missionaries further south

BURTON ONCE VISITED THE HOLY CITY OF MECCA DISGUISED AS AN ARAB.

heard rumors of a great inland sea that might flow out into the Nile River.

These tales fascinated English explorers Richard Burton and John Speke. As partners they trekked inland from Zanzibar to study Lake Tanganyika in 1856. On the way back, Speke went north and saw "a lake so broad you could not see across it, and so long that nobody knew its length." It was Ukerewe, the largest freshwater lake in the world.

Source of the Nile

Convinced he had found the Nile's source, Speke named it Lake Victoria (again after England's queen). But Burton

SINCE A DAM FLOODED THOSE FALLS DISCOVERED BY SPEKE AND GRANT, THE BUJAGALI FALLS 5 MILES (7.5 KM) DOWNSTREAM, MARKS THE NILE'S SOURCE.

43

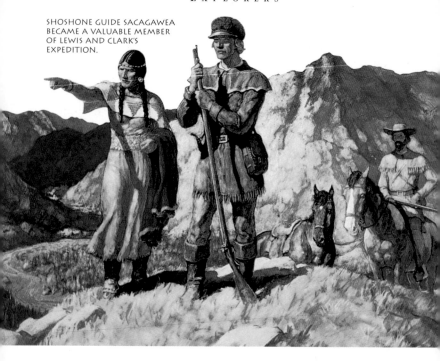

SHOSHONE GUIDE SACAGAWEA BECAME A VALUABLE MEMBER OF LEWIS AND CLARK'S EXPEDITION.

did not believe Speke, and the two men returned to England bitter rivals.

Speke went back in 1860, this time with James Grant. They found their way around the west side of Lake Victoria, and at the northern tip discovered a waterfall. There Speke wrote that "Old father Nile without any doubt rises in Victoria." He pressed on north, following the river wherever he could, as far as Juba in Sudan – the highest point to which the Nile had been explored from the other direction.

Burton never accepted Speke's claims, and the two men planned to present their arguments in a public debate in 1864. But on the day of the debate, Speke died in a shooting accident.

Speke was right – Lake Victoria is the source of the White Nile, but this was not finally proved until 1877, when British general Charles George Gordon mapped the river.

Crossing America

Africa was not the only continent to be explored by river. While Mungo Park was thrashing around in the Niger, two army officers were leading an epic journey across the

North American continent.

In 1803, US president Thomas Jefferson organized a group to explore the uncharted West of North America. He named this new group The Corps of Discovery, and put his secretary, Captain Meriwether Lewis, in charge. It took Lewis and his friend Lieutenant William Clark 28 months to reach the Pacific Ocean from St. Louis, Missouri, and return.

THE HIDATSA PEOPLE OF NORTH DAKOTA WARNED LEWIS AND CLARK ABOUT THE HUGE BEARS TO BE FOUND IN MONTANA.

They set off in May 1804, and followed the Missouri River upstream to its source in the Rocky Mountains. Once there, they unloaded the boats and used horses to carry their supplies as far as the Clearwater River. Building new boats there, they sailed downstream to join the Columbia River, reaching its mouth – and the Pacific Ocean – before returning along the Yellowstone River and rejoining the Missouri.

F riendly locals
Bad weather stopped Lewis and Clark's Corps of Discovery from traveling during the winter, so in the colder months they rested in camps. The first winter they spent as guests of the Mandan Sioux people, who treated them very well. It was a tradition of many Native American men to share all they had with their guests – their

WEIRD WORLD
WHILE IN MONTANA, SIX OF LEWIS AND CLARK'S EXPEDITION WERE CHASED INTO A RIVER BY A FEROCIOUS BROWN BEAR. IT TOOK MORE THAN FOUR BULLETS TO KILL THE ATTACKING BEAR.

food, their water, and even their wives! They also provided the explorers with a valuable guide and translator called Sacagawea, a Native American woman of the Shoshone people. She helped Lewis and Clark gain the trust of the Native Americans they met.

LEWIS AND CLARK ADMIRED THE LIGHT CANOES USED ON THE PACIFIC COAST.

Mapping America

Most of what the Corps of Discovery "discovered" was already known to Native Americans, and their tough journey was nothing like the easy river crossing of the continent they had hoped for. Nevertheless, to the European settlers, the 8000-mile (13,000-km) round trip was a spectacular achievement. Lewis and Clark charted the rivers they traveled and helped to draw up the first maps of the region. The trip also gave Americans a sense of the huge size and rich resources of this continent.

South America

Two weeks after Lewis and Clark had set off, US President Thomas Jefferson was having lunch with another famous explorer. His guest, Alexander Von Humboldt, was one of the greatest scientists of the age. Humboldt was on his way home to Germany from a five-year-long expedition in South

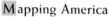

CANOES ARE THE MAIN FORM OF TRANSPORTATION ON THE ORINOCO; BUT UNLIKE HUMBOLDT'S, THEY ARE MOTORIZED.

America with his assistant Aimé Bonpland. Part of their mission had been to find out more about the wildlife of South America. They made some remarkable discoveries, but had a truly terrible time in the process! Insects and rain destroyed all their supplies, they nearly starved, they were almost drowned in the alligator-infested Orinoco River, and they had to brave earthquakes. However, it was insects that

SOME MOSQUITOES CARRY THE LIFE-THREATENING DISEASE MALARIA.

drove Humboldt absolutely nuts! They suffered so many insect bites that they could hardly move their hands.

Discovering rivers

Humboldt had many different goals during his South American explorations, but one of the most important was to investigate the Amazon and Orinoco river systems.

Traveling up the Orinoco, he discovered that the two rivers were linked by a third, the Casiquiare. He made this discovery only after a terrifying journey in a dugout canoe paddled by what Humboldt called "naked savages" – the native people of South America. Without these courageous and resourceful men, the two Europeans would have stood no chance in the river rapids, which flowed over gigantic granite boulders. River travel can be a tricky business!

DUSTY TREKS

The sun burns your face. You gasp from thirst. Your feet are blistered. But at the end of a vacation trek through a hot, barren land, you can at least look forward to a clean hotel and a cool shower. The first people to explore deserts and other such desolate landscapes were not so lucky.

MARCO POLO IN THE TRADITIONAL COSTUME OF THE TARTARS (ASIAN PEOPLE UNDER THE RULE OF GENGHIS KHAN)

Venetian voyager

In 1271 (when a long journey meant a trip to the next town), Venetian traveler Marco Polo crossed Asia with his father and uncle. Sounds like a cozy family vacation? Think again. There was trouble at every turn! First, near the Persian Gulf,

MARCO POLO WROTE ABOUT HIS TRAVELS WHILE IN PRISON

evil King Nogodar's bandits almost killed them. In Iran's desert, the only water was "bitter green stuff...if you drink a drop, it will set you purging 10 times at least." (No prizes for guessing what Polo meant by "purging"!) As if that weren't enough, in the Gobi desert, ghostly voices were said to call travelers by name, luring them away from their companions to a lonely death.

Chinese adventure

Marco Polo's trek took more than three years, but it was worth it! China's ruler, Kublai Khan, entertained the weary trio with a sumptuous feast, and made Marco Polo the governor of Yangzhou province. Marco must have liked China, for he stayed there 17 years. When he returned home, he astonished Venetians with stories of Chinese inventions such as coal fires, paper money, ice cream, and pasta.

Explorer or storyteller?

The Venetians called him "Marco di Millione." Why? Perhaps because there was

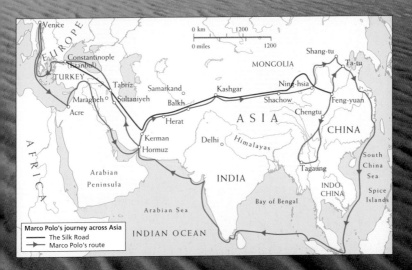

MARCO POLO'S JOURNEY STARTED IN VENICE. ONCE IN ASIA, HE FOLLOWED THE PATH OF THE SILK ROAD TO CHINA.

always a million of everything in his descriptions of China. Some say it was because he told a million lies. Even today, nobody is sure how much of Marco Polo's story is true. If he really went to China, why didn't he mention the famous Great Wall, or tea drinking?

On his travels through China, Marco Polo had one huge advantage – a golden tablet from Kublai Khan. This "passport" guaranteed him the emperor's protection.

Legendary city

Five centuries later something similar would have helped Frenchman René Caillié out of some nasty scrapes on his quest for Timbuktu. When Caillié's journey began in 1824, Europeans dreamed of visiting this mysterious desert city in

René Caillié
1799-1838
4.50 LA POSTE 1999
RÉPUBLIQUE FRANÇAISE

IN 1999, THE FRENCH POST OFFICE PRINTED A STAMP TO CELEBRATE RENÉ CAILLIÉ'S JUBILEE.

west Africa. Its Muslim inhabitants killed any Christian who reached it, but according to legend gold was as common there as iron was in Europe.

To visit Timbuktu and return alive, the daring adventurer had to dress, speak, and behave as if he were a Muslim. Even so, on the way there he was almost unmasked several times. On April 20, 1828, he got his first glimpse of the fabled city.

WEIRD WORLD

CAILLIÉ DINED ON MOUSE STEW, COMPLETE WITH THEIR TINY FEET, WHILE RESTING AT THE IVORY COAST TOWN OF TIEMÉ.

KNOWN AS "SHIPS OF THE DESERT", CAMELS CAN TRAVEL FOR MONTHS WITHOUT WATER.

A disappointing discovery

It was a dusty dump! Timbuktu was once a glorious capital of Islamic learning. But it had decayed into a run-down desert trading post. Stinking, mangy camels paced the sand-scrubbed streets. Disappointed, Caillié headed home – across the parched Sahara desert. This was a big mistake.

S weltering Sahara

The Frenchman spent the whole journey tormented by heat, thirst, and sandstorms.

Some of Caillié's companions were so thirsty that they drank their own urine, or bit their fingertips to drink the blood!

At the mid-Sahara oasis (watering place) of Telig, they had to dig out sand that had choked the water holes. When the camels smelled water, they fought for the first drink. Crazy with thirst, Caillié squirmed between the camels' legs and plunged his face into the salty pool, drinking with the animals. Caillié's journey from Telig to the safety of Fez in

TIMBUKTU WAS THE LAST TOWN TRAVELERS REACHED BEFORE HEADING NORTH ACROSS THE DESERT. FOR THOSE COMING SOUTH, IT MARKED A WELCOME END TO THE DESERT.

Morocco took a further 10 weeks. During the last punishing section of the trek, Caillié fell from a camel and almost broke his back.

To cross the Sahara, René Caillié had joined a caravan — a large group traveling together for safety. Its Arab leaders knew the best routes, and where to find water.

ALTHOUGH HIS EXPEDITION WAS A DISASTER, ROBERT BURKE (LEFT) HAD MADE THE FIRST RECORDED CROSSING OF AUSTRALIA.

with him William Wills, Charles Gray, and John King.

Across the Outback

However, the first European explorers to cross Australia's scorched interior did not have the same advantage. In 1860, Irish-born Robert Burke and his team set off from the southern port of Melbourne. They were headed for the Gulf of Carpentaria, some 1,400 miles (2,253 km) to the north.

Expedition's end

Sticky heat, squelchy mud, and annoying biting insects tortured the four, but on February 17, 1861, the expedition reached its goal on the north coast. It was on the return trip that trouble really started. As they trekked back south the food ran out, and they had to eat their horses, Boocha and Billy. Gray died despite the extra food. Burying him tired the other three, and delayed them by a vital day.

When they limped into

ABORIGINALS WERE THE FIRST INHABITANTS OF AUSTRALIA

The expedition soon ran into difficulties. Their leader, Burke, decided to split them up, leaving groups waiting in camps while he and a hand-picked few raced ahead. Only four explorers went beyond the fly-infested waterhole of Cooper's Creek. Burke took

Cooper's Creek, the survivors found an empty camp. Their comrades had left just hours earlier. The three men were too exhausted to follow. Hemmed in by desert on all sides, Burke and Wills eventually died. Native Australians nursed King until rescuers arrived.

B urke the hero

The Australian newspapers forgave Burke's bad leadership and cheered his "moral heroism." But King, they said, deserved credit only for his "physical endurance" because he was just a common soldier. In reality, Burke knew nothing about exploration and organized the trip very badly. It is said that in his job as a policeman, Burke often got lost in his own hometown!

LOG ON...
Find out more at:
www.burkeandwills.net

NATIVE AUSTRALIANS WERE EXPERTS AT SURVIVING IN THE PARCHED OUTBACK, BUT BURKE AND WILLS SCORNED THEIR SKILLS.

ICY ADVENTURES

The frozen parts at the top and bottom of the Earth were the last places to be explored – mainly because they were so hard to reach and bitterly cold. To 20th-century explorers, however, the north and south poles became great opportunities for fame and fortune. Their frosty attractions led to some of the most heroic and exciting journeys in history.

RUSSIAN ADVENTURER THADDEUS VON BELLINGHAUSEN WAS THE FIRST TO GAZE AT THE WEST COAST OF THE ANTARCTIC PENINSULA IN 1821.

The mysterious poles

Now, you might think that a continent bigger than Europe would be hard to miss, but Antarctica (the continent around the south pole) is a long way from anywhere. Mapmakers guessed it existed, but nobody actually saw this continent until 1820.

The Arctic ice cap (the north pole) is just one giant ice cube. To the Inuit and Sami people who lived on its edges, the Arctic was an empty wasteland, and they could not imagine why anyone would ever want to go there.

The Northwest Passage

It was the silks and spices of Asia that first lured European explorers to the Arctic. They figured that by sailing over the top of the world they could find a quick way to the East.

Floating ice blocked a direct voyage, so the search began for a Northwest Passage (route) around the top of what's now Alaska, and a Northeast Passage, around Russia.

Navigator John Cabot was the first to try the northwest route, when he sailed from England in 1497. Cabot reached North America, and thinking it was Asia's northwest coast, he returned triumphant. The following year, he set off on a second trip — and

HENRY HUDSON'S 1610 SEARCH FOR THE NORTHWEST PASSAGE ENDED WHEN HIS HUNGRY CREW MUTINIED AND SET HIM ADRIFT IN A SMALL BOAT.

disappeared. The Northwest Passage had claimed its first victim. Many more, mostly from Britain, were to follow.

Few did worse than Henry

CANNED MEAT POISONED MEMBERS OF FRANKLIN'S 1845 EXPEDITION. THE CANS LEAKED HIGH LEVELS OF TOXIC LEAD.

Hudson, who in 1610 sailed into the great bay named after him – only to be set adrift by his rebellious crew. Most later expeditions suffered terrible hardships, battling icebergs, fiendish cold, and disease. The crew of John Franklin's 1845 expedition even ate each other to avoid starvation. Roald Amundsen finally unlocked the Northwest Passage in 1906 when he sailed through the maze of islands to the Pacific. Amundsen's three-year voyage was heroic, but achieved little – the ice was too thick for regular shipping. Today, though, climate change is melting the ice, and the Northwest Passage may soon cut the sea journey from Europe to Japan by as much as 5,000 miles (8,000 km).

The Northeast Passage
Going the other way proved almost as hard. Englishman Hugh Willoughby had the first try at the Northeast Passage in 1553. He sailed around the top of Norway before freezing to death in the ice. After a couple more expeditions, the English got bored with the Northeast Passage, but the Dutch took over the hunt. In 1596, Dutch explorer William Barents got further around before ice trapped his ship. His crew built a hut and survived the winter, but Barents died before rescuers arrived in the spring.

LOG ON...
Find out about Franklin at:
www.ric.edu/rpotter/SJFranklin.html

THE SHELTER THAT BARENTS' CREW BUILT FROM THE WRECK OF THEIR SHIP WAS PROBABLY MUCH LESS COMFORTABLE THAN THIS IMAGINATIVE PICTURE SUGGESTS!

Russian travelers

Early explorers might have succeeded if they had used lighter ships. Around the same time as the Dutch and the English, Russian fur hunters were traveling all around the Russian Arctic in small ice boats called kochi. In 1648, navigator Semyon Dezhnev used these boats to lead 60 hunters round the right-hand end of Siberia and into the Pacific. He found the Northeast Passage without

NANSEN'S SHIP, THE FRAM, DRIFTED WITH ARCTIC ICE FOR THREE YEARS

even trying! However, this sea route to Asia was forgotten until 1728, when navigator Vitus Bering sailed through the passage of open water separating Asia and North America (the Bering Strait). Bering died on a second trip, but his voyages helped chart most of the Northeast Passage. Today, icebreakers stop the passage from freezing during summer so that ships can use it.

THE SPECIALLY STRENGTHENED HULL OF AN ICEBREAKER SLIDES UP ON THE ICE – THE SHIP'S WEIGHT THEN BREAKS A PASSAGE THROUGH.

To the north pole

The Northeast and Northwest passages were routes around the north pole. Nobody tried going to pole itself until 1879,

THE BOTTOM OF THE FRAM WAS CURVED TO DEFLECT THE PRESSURE OF THE ICE. AS THE POLAR SEA FROZE, IT LIFTED FRAM RATHER THAN CRUSHING IT.

when a small steamer, the *Jeanette*, set off from New York. Arctic ice soon crushed the ship and carried it 3,300 miles (5,400 km). The drifting wreck of the *Jeanette* gave Norwegian explorer Fridtjof Nansen an idea. "Why not build a ship strong enough to withstand the crushing pressure..." he thought "...and let the drifting ice transport it to the pole?" His ship, the *Fram*, set off from Norway in 1893. Nansen didn't reach the pole, but he got closer than anyone before.

One man was delighted Nansen had failed. American naval officer Robert Peary longed to be first to the pole. He and his friend, Matthew Henson, made their first unsuccessful attempt the same year as Nansen. Their expeditions in 1900 and 1902 also failed, but Peary would not accept defeat. He made clear just how determined he was when he suffered from frostbite. As Henson cut Peary's boots from his feet, the explorer's frozen toes snapped off like dry twigs. Peary shrugged, adding, "A few toes aren't much to give to achieve the pole."

The pole at last!

The two men tried again in March 1909. They set off with 19 sleds, 133 dogs, and 22 Inuit helpers. On April 6, at around 10 a.m., Peary estimated that they were near their goal. On the featureless ice, he used surveying instruments to take measurements of the Sun's position. When these confirmed that they

ALL HIS LIFE PEARY LONGED TO BE FAMOUS. HE SAW A TRIP TO THE NORTH POLE AS A WAY TO ACHIEVE HIS DREAM.

were at the top of the world, Peary wrote in his journal "The pole at last!...my dream and ambition for 23 years. Mine at last." But was it? For years afterward people questioned whether Peary had really reached the north pole first. Rival explorer Frederick Cook boasted that he had gotten there the year before. Today, few believe Cook's claim. An expert study in 1990 suggested that Peary had not cheated.

To the south pole

The other end of the planet was virtually unknown until the early 19th century. Then, all of a sudden in 1820, travelers from Britain, Russia, and the US all claimed the first sighting of the great southern continent. Seal and whale hunters nibbled at the edges

WEIRD WORLD
PEARY'S CLAIM THAT HE REACHED THE NORTH POLE WAS DOUBTED PARTLY BECAUSE ONLY INUITS AND HENSON, HIS AFRICAN-AMERICAN COMPANION, WENT WITH HIM. WIDESPREAD RACISM MEANT PEOPLE ONLY BELIEVED WHITE WITNESSES.

of Antarctica for the next 80 years, but the isolation of the place, and the ice surrounding it,

PEARY USED DOG SLEDS FOR TRANSPORTATION. TODAY THEY ARE MAINLY USED IN THE ARCTIC FOR SPORT.

made exploration horribly difficult. Serious attempts to reach the south pole began in 1909, when a British expedition led by Ernest Shackleton walked to within 100 miles (160 km) of it.

Shackleton's near-miss encouraged two rival explorers – Norwegian Roald Amundsen, and Briton Robert Scott. In 1911, both men sailed for the Antarctic. It would be a daring race for the south pole.

First to the pole

Unfortunately, it was a pretty unequal race. Skis and dog-sleds allowed the Norwegians to travel fast. The ponies on which Scott relied to carry supplies sickened and died, and the British had to haul their sleds by hand. Amundsen had organized plentiful supplies. Scott stockpiled barely enough for four men – then took four companions with him, not three as originally planned.

It's not difficult to guess who reached the pole first. The Norwegians set off two weeks before the British, and made it to the pole 10 days before Christmas. Scott arrived five weeks later. Finding a Norwegian tent and flag, he wrote in his diary "Great God!

THE COVER OF AMUNDSEN'S BOOK ABOUT THE RACE SHOWS THE NORWEGIANS TRIUMPHANT AT THE POLE.

This is an awful place…"

Sad ending Unfortunately worse was yet to come. Starving, cold, and tired, the five Britons began the 850 miles (1,350 km) return trip. One died after a month. When frostbite made another team member lame, he walked out into a blizzard and to his death rather than slow down the others. Despite this sacrifice, Scott and his two remaining companions died 12 days later. They were just 11 miles (18 km) from a depot of food and fuel that would have saved their lives.

Reaching the pole was the high point of Amundsen's career as a polar explorer, but it wasn't the end. He flew an aircraft across the Atlantic in 1925, and reached the north pole in a balloon the following year. His achievements made him a hero everywhere – except in Britain.

SCOTT AND HIS TEAM ARRIVED AT THE POLE TO FIND PROOF THEY HAD BEEN BEATEN – AMUNDSEN'S TENT.

ONWARD! UPWARD!

Exploring the Earth's surface doesn't have to mean going to places nobody has ever seen before. Exploration can also mean probing the extremes – the deepest, the coldest, the hottest, and the highest. Altitude – height above sea level – is a barrier that makes high mountain tops harder to explore than even the poles.

MOUNTAINEERS GRIP AND CUT STEPS WITH ICE AXES.

Ancient mountaineers

Climbing mountains just to get to the top is a fairly new idea. Until 300 years ago mountains were considered terrifying obstacles. People climbed around them, across them, but never up them. The discovery in 1991 of a frozen body on the Austrian/Italian border

SCIENTISTS WORKED OUT THAT ÖTZI'S BODY WAS 5,300 YEARS OLD

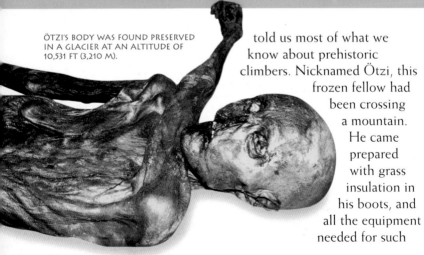

ÖTZI'S BODY WAS FOUND PRESERVED IN A GLACIER AT AN ALTITUDE OF 10,531 FT (3,210 M).

told us most of what we know about prehistoric climbers. Nicknamed Ötzi, this frozen fellow had been crossing a mountain. He came prepared with grass insulation in his boots, and all the equipment needed for such

MODERN MOUNTAINEERING BEGAN IN THE 18TH CENTURY WITH EXPLORATION OF EUROPEAN GLACIERS (RIVERS OF ICE).

a journey – a backpack, an ax, and a fur cloak were all found near his body. We're not sure exactly what Ötzi was doing on the mountain, but we know he was there for 5,300 years.

Some people became mountaineers by accident. Some 2,000 years ago, North African general Hannibal tried to cross Europe's Alps from France to Italy. Unlike Ötzi, Hannibal wasn't alone – following him were 120,000 troops and 37 elephants. (They were invading Italy). Hannibal's mountain crossing was a success, but mountaineering did not catch on immediately.

Climbing for prizes

It wasn't until the 18th century that mountain climbing as we know it became a popular sport. Horace de Saussure of Switzerland gave climbing a boost in 1760 when he offered a prize to the first person to climb Mont Blanc, the highest mountain peak in Europe, on the French/Italian border. De Saussure was a scientist, and he calculated that his money was safe for a while. But in 1786, a doctor from Chamonix, the town at the foot of the mountain, reached the top and claimed the prize.

A new sport

Over the next century exploring mountains became a pretty fashionable thing to

WHYMPER'S TWEED SUIT OFFERED LITTLE PROTECTION FROM ROCK FALLS ON THE MATTERHORN.

greater discomfort, and with the potential for much bigger, more dangerous falls! Alexander von Humboldt bravely climbed Mount Chimborazo in Ecuador, but for most climbers the Himalayas were the ultimate challenge.

The biggest challenge

The Himalayas mountain range divides China from India, and includes 11 of the world's 12 highest peaks. At 29,000 ft (8,800 m) Chomolunga was the tallest of all, but nobody knew this until India's British rulers ordered a survey of the region in 1852.

They promptly renamed the mountain after the chief surveyor, George Everest. Climbing Mount Everest wasn't going to be easy. It is so high that the air near the top contains hardly any oxygen – the life-giving gas

do, and, by 1865, there was just one European peak that remained unclimbed – the Matterhorn on the Swiss/Italian border. English artist Edward Whymper finally made it to the top, after trying seven times. However, Whymper's expedition ended tragically. On the way down four companions slipped and fell to their deaths.

Accidents like this were common, and soon falling from European mountains was becoming just too ordinary. Enthusiastic mountaineers began to look for other peaks which they could climb in

WEIRD WORLD
FROM THE SUMMIT OF THE MATTERHORN, EDWARD WHYMPER CELEBRATED HIS VICTORY BY PELTING ROCKS ON HIS RIVAL ITALIAN CLIMBERS BELOW!

we absorb when we breathe.

In 1922, a group of British climbers made the first attempt to climb Everest. Compared to today's mountaineers, they seemed hopelessly ill-prepared. Their tweed suits and sweaters were made for climbing English hills, not Asian mountains.

B ring your own air

They did get one thing right, though – they took along oxygen, compressed in metal cylinders. The expedition's porters, Sherpa people who lived on Everest's lower slopes, called the tubes "English air." The oxygen allowed climbers to go higher than ever before. However, problems with the breathing equipment forced them to turn back 1,300 ft (400 m) below the summit, and a storm killed seven Sherpas. A second British attempt two years later got higher still, but tragically the two climbers died trying to reach the summit of this great mountain.

FROM A DISTANCE, THE WORLD'S HIGHEST MOUNTAIN, EVEREST (LEFT), LOOKS SHORTER THAN ITS NEIGHBOR, NUPTSE, ON THE RIGHT.

LOG ON...
Find out more about Everest at:
www.nationalgeographic.com/everest

The British tried again in 1933, 1936, and 1938. They failed each time, defeated by weather, by exhaustion, by the thin air – or all three.

In 1952, the government of Nepal, which controlled the mountain's south side, decided to let another country have a try. A team of Swiss climbers

L ast chance to be first

For the British, of course, the Swiss defeat was a relief. They had always considered Everest "their" mountain (having made so many attempts), and the following year they got another chance. The British knew if they failed this time, climbers from another country would

THE SUMMIT OF EVEREST IS THE HIGHEST POINT ON EARTH

pioneered a new route up the mountain. They set a new altitude record, and almost got to the top. Unfortunately, in mountaineering, almost isn't good enough.

beat them to the top.

Expedition leader John Hunt picked the best climbers from Britain, New Zealand, and Nepal. In March 1953, they set off from Nepal's capital, Kathmandu. Their equipment was carried by 450 Nepali men and women. Reaching Everest the Sherpa porters moved all the supplies and equipment cautiously through the Khumbu Glacier. This frozen river was broken into a dangerous maze of ice blocks, some as big as houses. The mountaineers and their porters made a series of camps higher

HUNT'S TEAM CARRIED EVERYTHING THEY NEEDED ON THEIR BACKS, INCLUDING THE AIR THEY BREATHED.

and higher up the mountain. Higher still, the climbers followed the Swiss route over bare rock glazed shiny with ice. They camped on narrow windswept ledges in tiny tents. By May the summit was in sight, and Hunt picked two pairs of climbers from the team to try to reach it.

To the summit!

On May 26th, Charles Evans and Tom Bourdillon set off. Just 300 ft (90m) from the top they decided it was too risky to continue and climbed down. Three days later New Zealand climber Edmund Hillary and Sherpa Tenzing Norgay made a second attempt from a higher camp. Just before noon on May 29th they clambered exhausted to the summit. They had done it!

HILLARY AND NORGAY TAKE A BREAK AT 1,710 FT (5,200 M). THEY REACHED THE TOP OF EVEREST THE NEXT DAY.

OCEAN DEPTHS

Deep, dark, and often dangerous, the oceans are the last unknown places on Earth. Why? First, people are not well equipped for underwater life – they do not have gills like fish, and can only survive minutes under water. Second, water is heavy – until recently, no diver could go deeper than 246 ft (75 m). To withstand the pressure of all that water, and to be able to breathe for any length of time, explorers of the ocean depths needed some serious protection.

GERMAN WATCHMAKER AUGUSTUS SIEBE INVENTED THIS HEAVY DIVER'S HELMET IN ABOUT 1830. THE DIVER BREATHED AIR THROUGH A HOSE.

Breathing in bells

Water pressure didn't bother the first undersea adventurers because they only explored the shallows. When a Greek man held his breath to dive for sponges and pearls 2,500 years ago, he would rarely stay down longer than a couple of minutes. The invention of air-filled bells or barrels in the 1800s made deeper dives possible. Divers gulped lungfulls until the trapped air ran out. Little changed until the 19th century when divers began to wear large air-filled helmets. A pump on the surface refreshed the air inside, but the heavy pipe linking helmet and pump made the diver into a puppet on a string!

In 1943, French sailor Jacques Cousteau and engineer Emile Gagnan invented SCUBA: Self-

EQUIPPED WITH HIS AQUALUNG, JACQUES COUSTEAU MADE UNDERWATER FILMS, SHOWING THE OCEANS AS FISH SAW THEM.

WEIRD WORLD

DIVERS WHO SWIM VERY DEEP ABSORB NITROGEN GAS FROM THE AIR THEY BREATHE. THE GAS AFFECTS THEIR BRAIN, CAUSING "RAPTURE OF THE DEEP" – THEY BEHAVE AS IF THEY ARE DRUNK!

Contained Underwater Breathing Apparatus. By carrying a tank of compressed air, and breathing it through a special valve, divers could swim down to about 328 ft (100 m).

Beebe and Barton

Ocean explorers who wanted to go any deeper were about as free as a canned sardine, because to protect themselves from the crushing effects of water pressure, they had to sit inside a strong metal container. Americans William Beebe and Otis Barton built the first of these. Their "bathysphere" was little more than a large steel ball with a window. In 1930, the two men loaded the ball up with oxygen tanks and clambered through the window. Helpers then bolted

on the glass, and lowered the ball into the ocean just 10 miles (16 km) off a small island called Nonsuch on the coast of Bermuda.

Deep dive

As Beebe and Barton were lowered into the sea, water began leaking in, but still they continued. For the two men, it was a tight squeeze to fit had never been seen alive before. Later dives took the bathysphere to depths of 3,000 ft (900 m), but Beebe's adventures were too risky to continue. If the cable broke, his craft would sink like a stone, out of

BEEBE AND BARTON'S RECORD DIVE STOOD FOR 15 YEARS

in the bathysphere. Beebe remarked: "The longer we were in it, the smaller it seemed to get." In the cramped ball, both men's bodies soon became numb. So numb in fact that Beebe did not notice he was sitting on a wrench! Its outline was still visible on his rump four days later.

On this first dive, to a record 800 ft (240 m), Beebe watched fish that

ENGINEER OTIS BARTON BUILT THE DEEP-DIVING BATHYSPHERE WILLIAM BEEBE DREAMED UP.

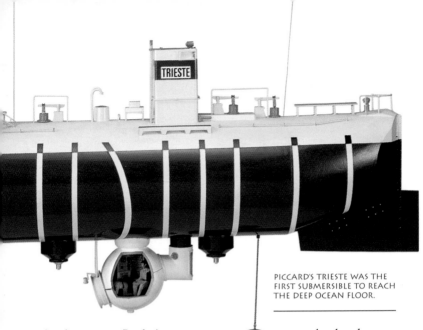

PICCARD'S TRIESTE WAS THE FIRST SUBMERSIBLE TO REACH THE DEEP OCEAN FLOOR.

reach of rescuers. Beebe's bathysphere was limited in another way – it could only move up and down, under the control of a winch on the mother ship above. Serious ocean explorers would need more mobile underwater craft – such as submarines.

Diving deeper

Submarines had been around since the 18th century, but they had one major drawback. They were designed to operate near the surface. It would take a very special kind of craft to dive to the ocean floor. In 1948, Swiss scientist Auguste Piccard built one. His bathyscaphe was Beebe's ball without string. To stop it from sinking uncontrollably, the round cabin hung below a giant float. Weights and electrically driven propellers allowed the craft to control its depth, and to move around underwater like a huge whale.

Piccard's craft – he built several of them – were the first of what we would now call submersibles. In 1953, one of them dived to 2 miles (3 km) in the Mediterranean Sea. Seven years later Piccard's son rode in the bathyscaphe *Trieste* nearly 7 miles (11 km) down to the deepest part of the deepest ocean – the Pacific.

Record-breaking vessel

The dive of the *Trieste* broke all records, but it did not actually tell us much about the ocean

73

Weird World

WORMS LIVING AROUND DEEP-SEA VENTS CAN WITHSTAND DRAMATIC HEAT CHANGES. ONE END OF THE WORM SURVIVES WATER NEAR BOILING POINT, THE OTHER END IS NEAR FREEZING.

a time into *Alvin's* cramped cabin for the past 35 years to dive as deep as 2.8 miles (4.5 km). Diving in 1985 with the similar French submersible *Nautile, Alvin* found the wrecked liner *Titanic,* which sank in the Atlantic Ocean in 1912.

Much more important for

floor that we didn't already know. For, by 1960, scientists had already found ways of exploring the ocean without getting wet feet. They had first mapped parts of it centuries earlier, by "sounding" (heaving overboard a weight on a long string). Later they used a technique called echo-sounding (making a "ping" noise and timing how long the echo took to return from the seabed) and satellite photography to map the oceans. Nevertheless, these techniques are no substitute for actually going down into the wet salty stuff; so despite the dangers, ocean exploration has continued in crewed craft.

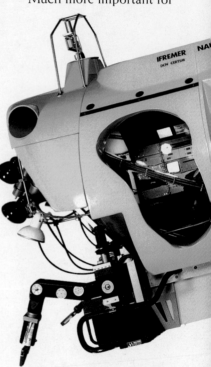

INSIDE NAUTILE (SHOWN HERE AS A MODEL) A CREW OF THREE CAN WORK ON THE OCEAN FLOOR FOR FIVE HOURS.

Super submersible

The best known of these is *Alvin*, a versatile submersible operated by Wood's Hole Oceanographic Institution of Massachusetts. Crew members have been squeezing three at

science was *Alvin's* discovery in 1977 of hydrothermal vents – hot springs on the ocean floor. Clustered around these hot spots in the otherwise chilly water was a thriving community of blind crabs, clams, and tubeworms – all of them previously unheard of. Submersibles such as the *Alvin* and the *Nautile* continue to make dives in a quest to find out more about the mysterious depths of our planet's oceans.

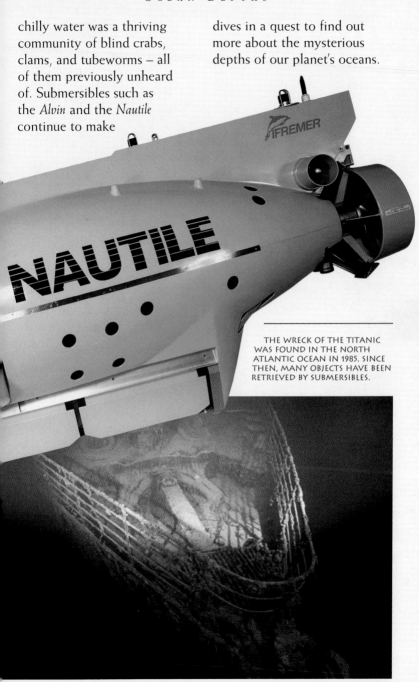

THE WRECK OF THE TITANIC WAS FOUND IN THE NORTH ATLANTIC OCEAN IN 1985. SINCE THEN, MANY OBJECTS HAVE BEEN RETRIEVED BY SUBMERSIBLES.

75

THE SPACE RACE

Exploring space was just a foolish fantasy until the 20th century. Then the invention of powerful rockets gave would-be space explorers a way to make their dreams come true. When a rocket launched the first satellite in the1950s, Russia and the United States became space rivals. The two countries competed to build the first spacecraft and to race them to the Moon.

The rocket engine
Space exploration is difficult because leaving Earth means overcoming gravity (the force that pulls everything toward the Earth's center). Rocket engines,

IN 1865 FRENCH STORYTELLER JULES VERNE WROTE ABOUT FIRING A MOON PROBE FROM A GIANT CANNON.

scientists made rockets into flying bombs, and fired them against their country's foe, Britain.

THE FIRST SPACE TRAVEL SOCIETY WAS FORMED IN GERMANY IN 1927

though, have enough power, and they can operate in the airless emptiness of space.

Liquid-fuel rockets were invented in the early 20th century, but at first they were used for warfare, not space exploration. During World War II (1939–45) German

After the war ended, the engineers continued their work in the United States, building much bigger rockets that were capable of pounding the United States' enemy, Russia. This provoked Russia to order even bigger rockets. This "mine's bigger than yours" game may seem childish, but it was deadly serious – and eventually led to the first voyages into space.

Early missions

In 1957 Russia used one of these huge missiles to launch into space the world's first artificial satellite, *Sputnik I.* It was little more than a metal beach ball that broadcast its temperature back to Earth in a radio bleep, but it scared and angered Americans. Fearful that Russia would dominate future space exploration, engineers from the United States hurried to build a spacecraft that could carry a human pilot.

Early plans were nicknamed "spam in a can" because the astronaut (the spam) simply sat helpless while the capsule (the can) hurtled around the Earth under rocket power. However, this was more white-knuckle ride than exploration, and the test-pilot astronauts wanted a craft they could fly. They eventually got their way – the first American capsules had jet engines so the astronauts inside could tilt or turn their tiny craft.

The first American in space

For a few nail-biting hours, it looked like they might not get the chance to use these craft. The first American space flight didn't start well.

On May 5, 1961, astronaut Alan Shepard was bolted into his capsule at the top of a tall rocket. He waited eagerly for the roar of engines to signal that his trip into space had begun. After minutes of delays stretched

GERMAN SCIENTISTS WHO BUILT THIS V2 MISSILE WENT ON TO BUILD SPACE ROCKETS FOR THE UNITED STATES.

"POYEKHALI" (LET'S GO!) SHOUTED THE WORLD'S FIRST SPACEMAN, YURI GAGARIN, AS HIS VOSTOK 1 ROCKET POWERED INTO ORBIT IN 1961.

into hours, Shepard's patience snapped. "Why don't you fix your little problem and light this candle!" he barked into the intercom. Eventually mission control did just that, and Shepard's spacecraft lifted successfully from the launch pad – to everyone's relief.

Russians race for first place
When Alan Shepard's capsule finally lifted from the launch pad, he made news headlines across the world. However, it didn't make the US the

winner in space. Just three weeks earlier the Russians had launched cosmonaut (Russian astronaut) Yuri Gargarin into orbit. Gagarin's capsule was more than three times bigger than Shepard's, and his flight lasted seven times as long. Gagarin had also made a complete orbit of the Earth, whereas Shepard just skimmed the edge of space. But, worst of all, Gagarin was first! It was a bitter blow to American pride.

A president's promise
Three weeks after Shepard's flight, president John Kennedy announced that NASA would send astronauts to walk on

the Moon within nine years. That was the easy part. He also promised to bring them back to Earth in one piece – a far more difficult challenge. With Kennedy's speech, true space exploration really began. American and Russian engineers raced to be first to the Moon.

In 1964, the Russians launched the first capsule with a multiastronaut crew. Five months later the US did the same. In March 1965 a Russian astronaut "walked"

In May, the US craft *Surveyor 1* did the same.

Race to the Moon

By 1968, though, NASA had taken the lead in the space race. Their Moon-landing program, named Apollo, was near completion. Missions 7, 8, 9, and 10 tested the spacecraft, but *Apollo 11* would be the mission to land Americans on the Moon.

The mission blasted off on

LOG ON...
Learn more about space at:
http://kids.msfc.gov/

NEIL ARMSTRONG SPENT 22 HOURS ON THE MOON

APOLLO 11

THE APOLLO 11 MISSION BADGE SHOWS AN AMERICAN EAGLE CARRYING AN OLIVE BRANCH TO THE SEA OF TRANQUILITY. THE OLIVE BRANCH IS A SYMBOL OF PEACE.

in space (safely attached to his capsule.) In June, an American repeated the feat. In January 1966, the Russian *Luna 9* craft made the first successful landing on the Moon's surface.

July 16, 1969, taking the crew of three on a four-day journey to the Moon. Once they had "parked" in Moon orbit, Neil Armstrong and Buzz Aldrin wriggled into the buglike lunar-landing craft *Eagle* and began their descent, while Michael Collins waited in the orbiting "mother ship," *Columbia*. The first part of *Eagle's* descent was automatic, controlled by a computer

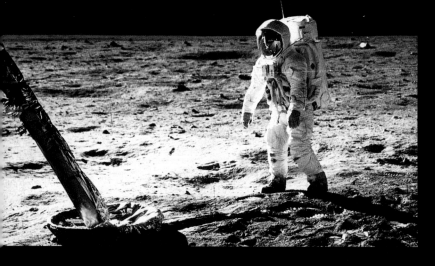

IN THE MICRO-GRAVITY OF THE MOON, NEIL ARMSTRONG WEIGHED LESS THAN A 10-YEAR OLD CHILD ON EARTH.

cruder than today's pocket calculator. Overloaded with data, it sounded warning alarms that nearly ended the mission. But technicians on Earth told Armstrong to ignore the alarms and press on. He took manual control and flew the craft to the landing site in the Sea of Tranquillity (actually a dusty plain). In a nail-biting landing, he touched down with just 30 seconds of fuel left.

One giant leap

Just before 4 a.m. on July 21, Neil Armstrong stepped

WITHOUT ATMOSPHERE OR WIND, AN ASTRONAUT'S FOOTPRINTS ON THE MOON WILL LAST A CENTURY.

out onto the Moon's surface in a cumbersome space suit. As he took his first step Armstrong made the now famous statement: "That's one small step for man, one giant leap for mankind." It was a moment of extraordinary and eerie excitement, broadcast live to 600 million TV viewers on Earth. Armstong and Aldrin planted the US flag in the soil of the Moon and collected rock samples. They stayed on the Moon for nearly a day before returning to *Columbia* to travel back to Earth. As promised, they returned safely, and to a heroes' welcome.

Was it worth it?

At enormous cost, the astronauts recovered a few buckets of stones. But the photographs they brought back were

WEIRD WORLD
ON THE GEMINI 3 FLIGHT, JOHN YOUNG PROTESTED ABOUT THE TASTELESS FOOD BY SMUGGLING ABOARD A CORNED-BEEF SANDWICH.

worth more than any dusty rock samples. For the *Apollo 11* astronauts recorded images of our Earth as we had never seen it before – rising behind the Moon's gray craters. Suddenly, our world seemed like a small and fragile globe, spinning in the dark vastness of space. These photographs brought new meaning and purpose to exploration. By studying our planet and its place in the universe, perhaps we can help preserve it for future generations.

THIS WONDERFUL "EARTHRISE" IMAGE WAS TAKEN BY ASTRONAUTS ON THE MOON.

FINDING THE WAY

The first explorers spent a lot of time getting lost. Sailors had the biggest problems – an hour's sailing was enough to take them out of sight of all landmarks. At first they used the stars, winds, and currents to guide them. Later inventions, such as the compass, made precise navigation possible; and today's travelers follow satellite beams.

Looking for landmarks
Before maps were created, overland travelers mostly relied on spoken directions to find their way. Maps, of course, are much more reliable than verbal directions – they can show mountains, rivers, coastlines, and other useful landmarks. Sea maps, or charts, showed

IN THIS 15TH-CENTURY PAINTING THE SAILORS ARE USING NAVIGATIONAL INSTRUMENTS TO GUIDE THEM AS THEY SAIL ACROSS THE INDIAN OCEAN.

LOG ON...
Find more navigation facts at:
www.istp.gsfc.nasa.gov/stargaze

coastlines, but mariners lost sight of land after just an hour or two's sailing. The deep ocean sailor's first real route-finding breakthrough was the compass. Attracted by the Earth's natural magnetism, a compass needle points north, so sailors can always tell which

THE VERY FIRST CHINESE COMPASSES HAD NEEDLES THAT POINTED SOUTH, NOT NORTH.

traveled north or south of the Equator. In the 13th century, Arab sailors were able to measure latitude with a kamal – a square of wood with a piece of string attached. Holding the string in their teeth, they aligned the wood square with a familiar star. Its height in the sky showed the latitude. Longitude – the distance sailed east or west – was more difficult. Sailors determined latitude from their speed, and their direction, which they knew from the

MAPS USED BY EARLY SAILORS WERE OFTEN INACCURATE

way they are heading. The compass was invented by the Chinese and used in the 4th century BC by Chinese travelers on land. European sailors didn't use the compass for another 1,600 years.

Latitude and longitude

You need more than a compass to find out exactly where you are – you need to know your latitude and longitude. Latitude is a measure of how far you've

compass. They guessed speed by throwing something off the bow (front) of the ship and counting the seconds until it floated past the stern (back).

Sea clocks

Clocks that took into account the rotation of the Earth greatly improved longitude measurements. Because the Earth turns once a day, the Sun changes position when you travel east or west. For each third of a mile (half kilometer) you go east, the time of sunrise (and sunset and noon) moves forward a second. So by knowing the clock time and comparing it to sundial time, you can figure out how far you've traveled.

The first accurate sea clock was invented in 1735 by John Harrison. With a Harrison "chronometer" 18th-century explorers were able to work out exactly where they were.

Modern navigation
Amazingly little changed until the 20th century, when the invention of radio provided new ways to avoid getting lost. During World War II

A GPS RECEIVER DISPLAYS LONGITUDE, LATITUDE, AND ALTITUDE (HEIGHT).

(1939–45) scientists developed radar, a system which relies on reflected radio beams to form a picture of a ship or plane's surroundings. Radio signals broadcast from a network of beacons on the ground enabled ships and planes near land to figure out their exact position.

The latest aids to navigation work almost everywhere on the globe. During the 1960s the US Navy launched a series of navigation

NAVIGATION SATELLITES BROADCAST THEIR SIGNALS FROM AN ORBIT 12,500 MILES (20,000 KM) ABOVE EARTH.

satellites into space. Any ship with he right equipment to receive radio signals from the satellites could instantly find its exact location and direction.

Today, 24 satellites provide a similar service to all travelers. With a global positioning system (GPS) receiver the size of a pocket calculator anyone can find their position with an accuracy of a few paces.

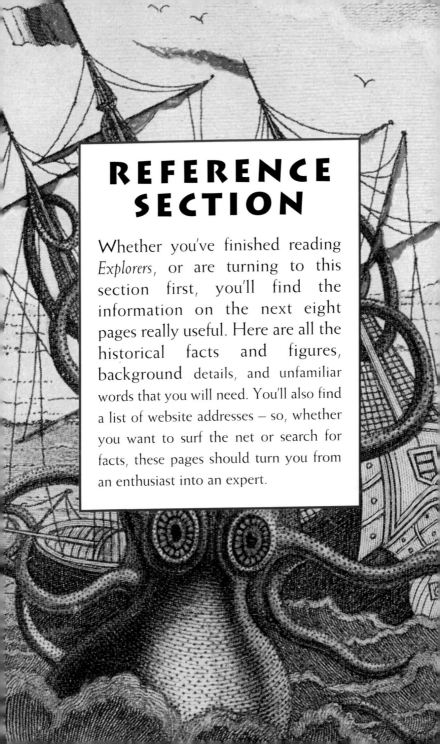

REFERENCE SECTION

Whether you've finished reading *Explorers*, or are turning to this section first, you'll find the information on the next eight pages really useful. Here are all the historical facts and figures, background details, and unfamiliar words that you will need. You'll also find a list of website addresses – so, whether you want to surf the net or search for facts, these pages should turn you from an enthusiast into an expert.

TIMELINE OF EXPLORERS

Alexander the Great
Macedonia 356–323 BC
Warrior-king who conquered and
explored the east Mediterranean
shore and west Asia.

Hannibal
Carthage (Tunisia) 247–181/3 BC
General who campaigned through
southern Europe and the Alps.

Chang Ch'ien
China d. 112/4 BC
Crossed Central Asia from eastern
China, returning via Tibet.

Fa-Hsien
China c.399–414
Buddhist monk who made a
pilgrimage to India and traveled
by sea to Sri Lanka and Java.

Hsüan Tsang
China 596–664
Buddhist explorer of Central Asia
whose wanderings took him as far
south as Madras in southern India.

Al Mas'udi
Iraq d. AD 957
Historian whose descriptions of his
travels became the Islamic world's
most important geography book.

Leif Eriksson
Norway AD 970
Viking who led the first European
expedition to North America
from Iceland.

Al-Idrisi
North Africa 1100–1166
Arab traveler and writer who visited
much of the Mediterranean.

Ch'ang-ch'un
China 1148–1227
Taoist monk who crossed Central
Asia from Peking to Afganistan
to visit Emperor Genghis Khan.

Marco Polo
Venice c.1254–1324
Explorer famous for his account of
his travels across Asia to the court
of China's Mongol emperor.

Ibn Battuta
Morocco 1304–69
Muslim religious judge whose
famous books describe his travels
in Asia, the Middle East, and Africa.

Cheng Ho
China 1371–1435 .
Naval commander who sailed the
Indian Ocean and the South China
Sea on ambitious trade missions.

Henry the Navigator
Portugal 1394–1460
Prince who first proposed sailing
around Africa into the Indian Ocean.

John Cabot
Italy c. 1450–c. 1499
Leader of the first British expedition
across the North Atlantic to
Canada's eastern tip.

Bartolomeu Dias
Portugal c.1450–1500
Navigator who was the first to sail
from the Atlantic to the Indian
Ocean around Africa's southern tip.

Amerigo Vespucci
Italy c.1451–1512
Navigator for whom America is

named. His voyages took him to the Caribbean and South America.

Diogo Câo
Portugal active around the 1480s
Explorer who sailed down most of Africa's Atlantic coast.

Christopher Columbus
Italy 1451–1506
First European navigator to reach the Americas.

Vasco da Gama
Portugal c. 1460–1524
Navigator who pioneered a sea route from Europe to India around Africa's southern tip.

Francisco Pizarro
Spain 1475–1541
Soldier who led the conquest of Peru's Inca people and claimed the country for Spain.

Ferdinand Magellan
Portugal c.1480–1521
Navigator who found the sea route from the Atlantic around South America to the Pacific Ocean.

Hernán Cortés
Spain 1485–1547
Soldier who led the conquest of Mexico's Aztec people and claimed the country for Spain.

Jacques Cartier
France 1491–1557
Sailor whose exploration of North America's Atlantic coast allowed France to claim and settle Canada.

Sir Francis Drake
England 1541–96
Naval captain and pirate who led the first English voyage of exploration around the world.

Hugh Willoughby
England d.1554
Led an early and disastrous search for the Northeast Passage. Willoughby disappeared during this voyage, and was later found dead.

William Barents
Netherlands c.1550–97
Navigator who died in his search for the Northeast Passage but who nevertheless added greatly to knowledge of the Arctic.

Henry Hudson
England 1565–1611
Navigator whose search for the Northwest Passage led to his death in the bay now named after him. Hudson's crew mutinied and set him adrift in a small boat.

Samuel de Champlain
France 1567–1635
Explorer of the St. Lawrence River and the eastern Great Lakes in Canada.

Abel Tasman
Netherlands 1603–c.1660
Navigator who explored the Indian Ocean and South Pacific and discovered Tasmania.

Semyon Dezhnev
Russia 1608–72
Explorer who was the first to pass through the Bering Strait, which links the Pacific and Arctic oceans.

Vitus Bering
Denmark 1681–1741
Navigator who helped chart Siberia's eastern tip and who sailed through the sea strait (now named after him) separating Asia from Alaska. Died on the return voyage from Alaska.

James Cook
England 1728–79
Navigator who made three epic
voyages of discovery, exploring
much of the Pacific Ocean.

**Alexander von Humboldt and
Aimé Bonpland**
Germany and France
1769–1859 and 1773–1858
Naturalists who together explored
Brazil's great rivers and climbed
peaks in the Andes. Alexander von
Humboldt became the greatest
scientist of his day.

Mungo Park
Scotland 1771–1806
Surgeon who twice explored the
Niger River in West Africa, dying
on the disastrous second trip.

**Meriwether Lewis and
William Clark**
US 1774–1809 and 1770–1838
Leaders of the first overland
expedition by European settlers
across the Rocky Mountains to
North America's West Coast.

Matthew Flinders
England 1774–1814
Explorer who sailed right around
Australia and charted (mapped)
much of the coast.

Ross, John and James
Britain 1777–1856 and 1800–62
Uncle and nephew who together
searched for the Northwest Passage.
James Ross also explored Antarctica.

John Franklin
Scotland 1786–1847
Navigator whose 1845 expedition
later led to the discovery of the
Northwest Passage.

René Caillié
France 1799–1838
First European to travel to the
Muslim city of Timbuktu and
return alive.

John Frémont
US 1813–1890
Mapmaker who became famous for
his bold exploration of America's
western frontier lands.

David Livingstone
Scotland 1813–73
Missionary and antislavery
campaigner who explored widely in
southern and central Africa. Named
the Victoria Falls in Zimbabwe.

Richard Burton and John Speke
England 1821–90 and 1827–64
Explorers who teamed up to search
for the source of the Nile River in
east Africa. Speke was later more
successful and proved that Lake
Victoria was the Nile's source.

Edward Whymper
England 1840–1911
Artist who led the first ascent of the
Matterhorn in the Swiss/Italian Alps
in 1865. Whymper was aided by
Swiss guide Michel Croz.

Henry Morton Stanley
Wales/US 1841–1904
Journalist and adventurer whose
explorations in Africa famously
included a successful search for
David Livingstone.

**Robert Peary and
Matthew Henson**
US 1856–1920 and 1866–1955
Explorers who led the first trip
across the Arctic ice to the
North Pole.

Fanny Workman
US 1859–1925
Traveler and mountaineer famed for her unconventional cycle tours. Her climbs in the Himalayas set records.

Robert Burke, William Wills, Charles Gray, and John King
Australia
Explorers who, led by Burke, made the first south to north crossing of Australia in 1860–1.

Fridtjof Nansen
Norwegian 1861–1930
Arctic explorer who made the first crossing of Greenland, and who championed the use of Inuit and Sami technology for polar survival.

Mary Kingsley
England 1862–1900
Traveler who explored West Africa without other Europeans, at a time when no other women did this.

William Beebe
US 1867–1962
Scientist who, with Otis Barton, made a world-record dive of 3,028 ft (923 m) in 1934 in a submersible they had built together.

Robert Scott
England 1868–1912
Naval officer whose expedition was the second, after Norwegian Roald Amundsen's, to reach the South Pole. Captain Scott died with all his men on the return trip.

Roald Amundsen
Norway 1872–1928
Navigator and explorer who was the first to sail through the Northwest Passage, and who led the first expedition to the South Pole.

Ernest Shackleton
Ireland 1874–1922
Antarctic explorer whose 1909 expedition came to within 100 miles (160 km) of the South Pole.

Auguste and Jean Piccard
Switzerland 1884–1962 and 1922–
Father and son who collaborated to build the first deep-sea submersible. Auguste also pioneered balloon ascents in the upper atmosphere.

Edmund Hillary and Tenzing Norgay
New Zealand and Tibet 1919– and 1914–86
Climbers, who in 1953, were the first to reach the top of Everest, the world's highest mountain.

Alan Shepard
US 1923–98
The first American to travel in space in 1961, Alan Shepard later commanded the *Apollo 14* mission to the Moon in 1971.

John Glenn
US 1921–
Test pilot John Glenn was the first American to make an orbital flight around the Earth in 1962.

Yuri Gagarin
Russia 1934–1968
The first human to fly in space, Gagarin made his single historic orbit of the Earth in 1961.

Neil Armstrong, Buzz Aldrin, and Michael Collins
US
Astronauts who in 1969 traveled to the Moon as crew of the *Apollo 11* mission. Armstrong was the first human to walk on the Moon.

EVEREST FACTS

1922 First attempted climb
A British team get to within
1,740 ft (530 m) of the summit.

1953 First successful attempt
A British-organized expedition
reaches the summit. New Zealand
climber Edmund Hillary and Sherpa
Tenzing Norgay climb to the top.

1975 First ascent by a woman
Women climbers in separate
Chinese and Japanese expeditions
reach the top.

1978 First ascent without oxygen
Italian Reinhold Messner and
Austrian Peter Habeler reach the
summit without using bottled oxygen.

1980 First solo ascent
Reinhold Messner was the first
to reach the top on his own and
return safely.

How tall is it?
The Survey of India calculated
Mount Everest's height as 29,002 ft
(8,840 m) in 1852. The next major
survey, a century later, came up with
a height of 29,028 ft (8,848 m).
The most recent, and probably
most accurate, measurement was in
1999. An expedition sponsored by
National Geographic and the Boston
Museum of Science measured the
height, using the latest satellite
equipment, as 29,035 ft (8850m).

POLAR FACTS

How cold is the South Pole?
The pole is on the Antarctic ice
cap at an altitude of 9,525 ft
(2,900 m) Nowhere on Earth is
colder. Temperatures fall as low
as to -129 °F (-89 °C).

**1820 First to sail around
Antarctica**
Fabian Bellinghausen sails around
Antarctica on the Russian ships
Vostok and Mirny.

1908 Furthest south
Irish explorer Ernest Shackleton
sleds to within 100 miles (160 km)
of the South Pole.

1911 First to reach South Pole
Roald Amundsen successfully leads
a Norwegian team to reach the
South Pole.

**1929 First flight over the
South Pole**
American Richard Byrd flies over
the South Pole as part of a huge
US Navy expedition, which also
mapped large areas of the continent.

**1957–8 First crossing of
Antarctica**
Vivian Fuchs leads a British
expedition across Antarctica
in tracked vehicles.

SPACE FACTS

First artificial satellite
The Russian *Sputnik* satellite was launched on October 4, 1957, and orbited the Earth for three months.

First animal in space
Space dog Laika volunteered to be the first living thing in space by foolishly wagging her tail at Moscow stray dogs' home when space engineers visited. She and 37 fleas were launched into orbit on November 3, 1957, aboard *Sputnik 2* to test the life-support systems before sending a human into space.

First crewed flight
Russian spaceman Yuri Gagarin was launched into space aboard the *Vostok 1* craft on April 12, 1961. He spent nearly two hours in orbit.

First woman in space
Russian spacewoman Valentina Tereshkova soared into space aboard *Vostok* on June 16, 1963. Her mission lasted three days.

First trip to the Moon
The *Apollo 10* mission, launched on May 18, 1969, flew three American astronauts to the Moon, and brought them safely back to Earth.

First Moon landing
US astronaut Neil Armstrong was the first human to set foot on the Moon when he stepped out on July 21, 1969, as part of the *Apollo 11* mission.

Longest time spent in orbit
Vladimir Titov and Musa Manarov boarded the Russian *Mir* space station on December 21, 1987, and stayed for 366 days.

First space station
On June 7, 1971, three Russian spacemen joined the orbiting *Salyut 1* space station. Though they carried out successful experiments for nearly a month, all three tragically died in an accident on their return to Earth.

Most distant part of the solar system visited
The furthest that human explorers have gone from Earth is the far side of the Moon, some 240,000 miles (386,000 km) away.

Speed needed to escape Earth's gravity
To lift a spacecraft into orbit, a rocket must be traveling at more than 7 miles (11 km) a second – 40 times faster than a jet airliner.

Survival time in space without a suit
Without a suit to provide protection and oxygen, astronauts would become unconscious in less than a quarter of a minute and would die in less than four minutes.

GLOSSARY

Altitude The height of a place measured from sea level.

Astronaut American term for any crew member on a spacecraft.

Bathyscaphe *See submersible*

Bathysphere A sealed diving capsule in which explorers are lowered into the ocean on the end of a cable.

Cape An area of land, sticking out into a sea or lake.

Compass Navigation device containing a magnetic needle that always points in the same direction.

Continent One of the Earth's seven great areas of land.

Desert An empty area of land where little grows because of extreme heat, cold, or dryness.

Equator An imaginary circular line around the Earth's middle, midway between the North and South poles.

Glacier A river of snow and ice that flows very slowly down a mountain.

Icebreaker A ship with a strong hull and powerful engines that can sail through sea ice.

Lunar Anything connected with the Earth's Moon.

Mountaineer Someone who climbs mountains, usually for enjoyment.

Navigation Finding or plotting the correct route.

Northeast Passage A sea route from the Atlantic to the Pacific around the north coast of Asia.

Northwest Passage A sea route from the Atlantic to the Pacific Oceans around the north coast of North America.

Oasis A place in the desert where water can be found.

Orbit To move in a circular path around the Earth, without falling to the ground or flying off into space.

Pole The most northerly and southerly points on Earth.

Rapids The shallow part of a river where the current is strong and the water flows quickly over rocks.

Rocket An engine which releases a jet of hot gas, used to launch spacecraft and missiles.

Sandbank A shallow sandy area of the ocean where ships risk running to ground and wrecking.

Sounding Measuring the water's depth using a weight on the end of a rope.

Space The vast, mostly empty, region in which the Sun, Earth, and all stars exist.

Strait A narrow channel linking two larger water areas.

Submarine Short for submarine boat, a warship that operates underwater.

Submersible A small craft that operates underwater without cables or pipes linking it to the surface.

Summit The highest point or top of a mountain.

EXPLORERS WEBSITES

National Geographic Society
The world's largest scientific and educational society, NGS supports scientific expeditions worldwide.
www.nationalgeographic.com/kids
1145 17th Street N.W.
Washington, D.C.
20036-4688

Royal Geographic Society
Royal Geographical Society is still one of the most active organizations supporting geography and exploration.
www.rgs.org
1 Kensington Gore,
London, SW7 2AR
United Kingdom
Email: membership@rgs.org

British Antarctic Survey
This scientific organization sponsors research and surveying in Antarctica and related regions.
www.antarctica.ac.uk
High Cross, Madingley Road
Cambridge, CB3 0ET
United Kingdom
E-mail: information@bas.ac.uk

Scott Polar Research Institute
The oldest international research center in the world covering both the Arctic and Antarctic regions.
www.spri.cam.ac.uk
University of Cambridge
Lensfield Road, Cambridge
CB2 1ER, United Kingdom

National Maritime Museum
The largest of its kind in the world, this museum mounts regular exhibitions about ocean exploration, some of which feature on its website.
www.nmm.ac.uk/

Smithsonian Institution
America's National Museum of Natural History regularly covers explorers and their achievements on its many web pages.
www.mnh.si.edu

European Voyages of Exploration
An award-winning website from the Applied History Research Group at the University of Calgary, Canada.
www.acs.ucalgary.ca/HIST/tutor/eurvoya/

The Age of Exploration
A guide to maritime discovery from ancient times to Captain Cook's 1768 voyage to the South Pacific,
www.mariner.org/age/index.html

The history of navigation
An in-depth look at the history of navigation from using the stars to modern GPS. Illustrated with detailed diagrams.
www.boatsafe.com/kids/navigation.htm

Antarctica panorama
A virtual tour of the South Pole base with details on how to get there and great photographs of the pole.
http://astro.uchicago.edu/cara/vtour/

Everest information
A good source of information ranging from history, folklore, natural history, and the practicalities of climbing the world's highest mountain peak.
www.pbs.org/wgbh/nova/everest

INDEX

CREDITS

Dorling Kindersley would like to thank:

Almudena Diaz and
Nomazwe Modonko for DTP
assistance. Thanks also to
Chris Bernstein for the index.

Additional photography by:
Peter Anderson, Geoff Brightling,
Tina Chambers, Steve Gorton,
Frank Greenaway, Alan Hills,
Dave King, Ian O'Leary, Neil Lukas,
Ray Moller, Susanna Price,
James Stevenson, Harry Taylor.

Picture Credits

The publishers would like to thank
the following for their kind permission
to reproduce their photographs:
c = center; b = bottom;
l = left; r = right; t = top.

AKG London: 29, 57br, 85.
Ancient Art & Architecture Collection: 1,
13, 31.
The Art Archive: Marine Museum
Lisbon / Dagli Orti 34; Richmond Borough
Council / Eileen Tweedy 43tr; University
Library Geneva / Dagli Orti 65.
Bridgeman Art Library, London /
New York: Bibliotheque National, Paris,
France, *Following the stars by Livre des Merveilles*
(c.1407–13) 82; British Library, London,
UK, *Sphera in Plano, from "Tolome Della Gegraf"*
28, *Vasco da Gama, illustration by Pedro Barretti
de Resende* 32; Museo Correr, Venice, Italy,
Marco Polo by Italian School (18th C.) 48cr;
Private Collection/Index, *The Landing of
Christopher Columbus by Spanish School*
(19th C.) 22; Royal Geographical Society,
London, UK, *Equipment from the 1953 Everest
Expedition* 68.
British Museum: 26–27c.
Corbis: Bettmann Archive 72; Hulton-
Deutsch Collection 40c, 77; Galen Rowell
58–59; Brian Vikander 39; Ralph White
75b.
Mary Evans Picture Library: 36, 38, 46t,
51, 56, 59tr, 63t, 66, 76.
Getty Images Stone: Nabeel Turner
19–20b.

Robert Harding Picture Library: 5, 61;
Rob Cousins 46–47; Alain Evrard 17;
Geoff Renner 3, 54–55.
Hulton Archive: 62–63.
Hutchison Library: S. Erring 48–49;
Crispin Hughes 20–21; R. Ian Lloyd 53;
Sarah Murray 12b.
Kobal Collection: 71.
N.A.S.A.: 79, 80bl, 80–81, 80t.
National Maritime Museum: 4, 14–15,
21tr, 33, 57tl, 83, 86–87, 88–89, 92–93.
Natural History Museum: 10.
Peter Newark's Pictures: 26b, 27tr, 44,
52, 60.
N.H.P.A.: Steve Robinson 42–43.
Pictor International: 25, 40–41, 67.
Pitt Rivers Museum: 12tr.
Popperfoto: Werner Nosko / Reuters.64b.
Musee de la Poste, Paris, France: 50t.
Roskilde Viking Ships Museum: 24.
Royal Geographical Society: Gregor 69.
Science & Society Picture Library:
De Astro Space 84cr.
Science Museum: 11tl, 73.
Science Photo Library: Novosti 78,
John Reader 11b.
Stock Market: David Keaton 9.

Book Jacket Credits
Front cover, background
Mountain Camera / John Cleare
Back cover, bl, tl
National Maritime Museum

All other images © Dorling Kindersley.
For further information see:
www.dkimages.com